The Pagan-Christian
Connection
EXPOSED

The Pagan-Christian
Connection
EXPOSED

Michael Rood

BRIDGE
LOGOS

Newberry, FL 32669

Bridge-Logos
Newberry, FL 32669

The Pagan-Christian Connection Exposed
by Michael Rood

Copyright ©2004 by Bridge-Logos

Library of Congress Catalog Card Number pending
International Standard Book Number 978-0-88270-520-0

Unless otherwise noted, all Scripture is from the King James Version of the Bible.

BP 02-01-17

Dedication

Jamie ... Words cannot convey my gratitude for your years of difficult and faithful service. Let the words of this book, which represent a fraction of our years of toil and tears together, be a token of my respect for you. No one has greater reason to appreciate you. I dedicate this book to you.

Acknowledgments

I AM indebted to many people who labor with me to cause "A Rood Awakening!" to occur in the lives of millions, just as the Almighty caused the same awakening in my own life. All these Saints found their voices to the world fulfilled in our mission to awaken the world to the truth of the Hebrew Scriptures and to His message of hope. This is "their" ministry and whether I live or die, their ministry would continue in much the same way as it now is—but probably much easier ...

Chaim Goldman, the multi-talented Israeli producer of our "A Rood Awakening!" television series, who has worked tirelessly for years on a project that is now changing the lives of millions around the world.

Linda Miller, my faithful secretary, who fulfilled her personal ministry as my liaison with believers around the globe. She passed away the month this book was released.

Don Visser, our U.S. production manager, who oversees the www.ARoodAwakening.tv website and distribution office—and has pulled us out of the fire on more than one occasion.

Roberto Umana, my eloquent Spanish voice for "Un Rood-o Despertar" and faithful companion in Israel.

The newest addition to the team, Beverly Browning, the editor for Bridge-Logos who turned my tedious tirades into poetic pugnacity.

Table of Contents

Preface

When Michael Rood walks onto a stage, the audience sees a bearded man in the sandals, tunic and robe from a place and time that seem far from the here and now. His formal appearance and humble introduction disarm the interested observer, for in the next split second, Michael shifts into high gear, grabs you by the hand, leads you on a journey back through your Bible, shakes you to the foundations of your soul, and changes you forever. Little wonder his audiences have come to refer to his message as, "A Rood Awakening!"

Michael Rood is a theologian, scholar, Bible teacher, researcher, media personality, and storyteller who has devoted his life to teaching the fulfilled prophecies of the Messiah—from a Jewish perspective. For years, this former U.S. Marine has been on a mission from his home in Israel. He has dared to go where few men have gone (geographically and theologically) to challenge long-held beliefs about the Bible and to guide all "who have ears to hear" to its historically accurate interpretation and understanding.

His bold, hard-hitting style is both spellbinding and shockingly honest as he opens the Scriptures to prophecies that you may have heard all your life, but never truly understood. His teachings are backed up by Scripture and well-researched historical and archaeological data, leaving no doubt that you will need to reconsider many of your beliefs. Now, after instructing more than 200,000 people at his "A Rood Awakening!" seminars, and reaching many more through international television, audio and video tapes, DVDs and radio shows, Michael Rood now brings his unique teachings to the pages of this book. This is the paradigm shift for which you have been waiting an entire lifetime. Prepare for "A Rood Awakening!"

This book is based on the television series, "A Rood Awakening!" filmed in the land of Israel where the author lives. The book tells a story that runs through the pages of the Hebrew Scriptures like a golden thread. The text is not encumbered with footnotes to prove every mundane point— as is commonly found in western exegetical literature. Rather, the story is told in a factual manner from a perspective that can only be realized by living in the land of the Bible. Most of the information presented in this volume is common knowledge among those who live in Israel and the Middle East, yet foreign to those who are 10,000 miles and 2,000 years removed from the language, culture, and people of the Bible. Sit back, relax, and enjoy the journey.

Introduction

Nearly 2,000 years ago, on the Day of Pentecost [the Feast of Shavuot], the Holy Spirit was poured out upon the Jewish followers of Y'shua on the Temple Mount. From that day until the household of Cornelius heard the Word of truth from the mouth of Peter, there were few, if any, Gentile followers of the Jewish Messiah. But, in those first 15 years, there were a myriad of Jewish followers of the Messiah, and a great company of priests—*Cohanim* who were obedient to the faith (Acts 6:7). After the Jewish believers realized that the Gentiles could come to Messiah without having to become proselytes to Judaism first, they gave their lives to get the good news out to the Gentiles. Who could have expected that after all of this time, there would be so many Gentile followers of the Jewish Messiah?

Now, those who are followers of the Messiah are one big happy family in Messiah. There are some things on which we will probably disagree, just as in every family. I suggest that if you and I can't find something to disagree on within the first three minutes of meeting each other, neither one of us is very intelligent, but that, of course, is not our goal. It is often observed, "If you have two Jews in a room, you're going to have at least three opinions." But at the end of heated disagreements we can agree that, "When the Messiah comes, He will interpret these things." We remain friends, and will meet again to fight another day.

I have maintained very strong convictions on both sides of so many arguments at different times in my life, that I can appreciate the plethora of personal opinions that I regularly encounter. I have heard it said on too many occasions, "Everyone is entitled to his own opinion." In a court of jurisprudence this statement simply means, "Ignorance and stupidity are insufficient grounds for capital punishment." It does not indicate that anyone's opinion is valid or even sane. Everyone is responsible for living out the instructions of the Creator according to the dictates of his own conscience, according to the leading of the Spirit of the Holy One by His revealed Word. I would like to assure you that you are not required to agree with me on everything I write in this volume. I seldom agree with *myself* on everything. But, I do not currently hold a single opinion that I think is wrong. I do feel very strongly that *you* are entitled to *my* opinion.

I invite you to leave your modern, Western Gentile mentality behind as we explore the Scriptures from a Hebrew perspective. This is the paradigm shift for which you have been waiting an entire lifetime. As the prophets said, the Gentiles will come to the believers among the Jews in the last days, take hold of the blue fringe on the corners of their garments and say, "Teach us the ways of the LORD, we now understand that the living oracles of GOD were committed to the Jews, and we have inherited nothing but lies and pagan gods from our forefathers—teach us about the Messiah" (Zechariah 8:23, Jeremiah 16:19).

Come home with me to the ancient Land of Israel. These

may be your first steps down this path, but I assure you, that this will be the adventure of your life.

Michael Rood

BOOK ONE

Sodom and Gomorrah Revisited

CHAPTER ONE

Sodom and Gomorrah

A Visible Example of GOD's Judgment and Mercy

Straddling an ancient stone wall that dropped to the ravine several thousand feet below, I rested from my exhausting pre-dawn trek up the side of the mountain. The sun peeked above the mountains of Seir and flashed across the waves of the Dead Sea. Below me, at the foot of this mountain fortress, several stone-cordoned encampments of the Roman army broke the desert into a checkerboard. Masada, the ruins of a once elaborately appointed Herodian refuge, now stands as a monument to Jewish resolve; what happened here in the days of Rome will not happen again!

It was here on Herod's veranda that a band of Jewish Zealots watched as Jewish slaves were forced by whip and chain to build a ramp for their Roman conquerors. That earthen ramp, once completed, would direct a monstrous siege engine up the backside of the mountain to the wall of Masada. That ramp would lead to the deaths of these freedom fighters, the defiling of their wives and daughters, and the

Masada, the ruins of a once elaborately appointed Herodian refuge, now stands as a monument to Jewish resolve.

lifelong enslavement of their sons to the Roman Empire. The Zealots on the mountaintop would not assault their Jewish brothers who, under duress of torture, were building the road to their destruction. The slaves who refused to be party to the project were commonly made public examples by being nailed to a Roman cross at the work-site. Over the next several days, they were roasted to death under the scorching desert sun.

It was here, on Herod's veranda, that the Zealots made their last stand for freedom and decided that they would mercifully end the lives of their friends and families rather than be subject to the cruelty of Rome. On the morning that the Romans broke through the wall, they realized a bitter victory. The Zealots had taken their own lives; they had put each other to a more merciful sword, rather than suffer brutalization at the hand of their conquerors. There were no survivors over whom Rome could celebrate their victory. After months of siege, the campaign was closed without pageantry, and Rome quickly evacuated the camps that now remain below me on the Dead Sea Valley floor. It is here on Masada that Israeli military forces are sworn to the resolve that there will never be another Masada.

The rocks below blurred as a motion picture played in my mind. The blistering sun rose higher in the sky as the 112-degree "breeze" whipped my sweat-soaked beard across my sunburned face. I would need to wait until sundown before starting the trek that had brought me to this remote pinnacle. I surveyed the deserted western plain, making a crude map of my proposed insertion point into the desert. The site I had come to inspect was flanked on the highway by red military signs stenciled with "DANGER MINEFIELD" and skull and crossbones. My experience as a United States Marine, guarding the Naval base at Guantanamo Bay, Cuba, suggested that the site I was preparing to inspect was on the border of a defensive minefield. Uncertain about the levels of security and surveillance I might encounter by trespassing into this area, I carefully noted the frequency of the motorized military patrols in the distance. I would not be deterred from the goal that had taken me halfway around the Earth: the search for the ashen remains of the city of Gomorrah on the Dead Sea Valley plain.

The Dead Sea is the lowest point on Earth and was once described by Moses as a well-watered plain "like the garden of the LORD."

Shore of the Dead Sea

Nearly 4,000 years ago, the crust of the Earth split open, forming the Great Rift Valley that cuts its jagged swath from Turkey—deep into the continent of Africa. Out of that fracture in the Earth's crust belched fire and brimstone that rained down upon the four cities that were built on the western plain—Sodom, Gomorrah, Admah, and Zeboim.

Genesis, the first book of Moses, records that Abraham stood in the door of his tent on the other side of the mountain upon which I sat, and watched as the cities and their inhabitants were incinerated in the inferno. Beyond my view from the distant north end of the Salt Sea, the Jordan River continues to wash minerals from the highlands of Israel into this dead end chasm. At the base of the mountain, out in the middle of the sun-parched Israeli desert, the remains of an ancient city still stand. This city, incinerated in an inferno nearly 4,000 years ago, is still covered with millions of chunks of highly flammable brimstone.

Abraham Leaves Babylon

In the book of Genesis we read that GOD instructed Abraham to leave the land of Babylon and its perverse system of *sun god* worship initiated by Nimrod. The Almighty had already confused the languages and scattered the inhabitants of Babylon into the far corners of the Earth—to slow down the development of Nimrod's political, economic, and religious

4

system of world government. The worship of Nimrod, who was reincarnated as Tammuz (the illegitimate son of Nimrod's widow), and the worship of Nimrod's wife (reincarnated as Ishtar—the queen of heaven) were both fragmented as divergent cults evolved from the confusion of languages at the Tower of Babel. Worship of Nimrod, Tammuz, and Ishtar continued in their original forms and traditions, but under a multitude of names. For thousands of years, religiously motivated military campaigns kept these once unified peoples from joining forces to rebuild the one world government that Nimrod had begun.

Raised in the land of Shinar, Abraham was instructed to leave his family, culture, and nation behind and to cross over the Euphrates River into a land that GOD would give his descendants. Abraham became the first *Hebrew* (meaning, "to cross over") when he crossed over the Euphrates River, leaving Babylonian paganism far behind. The Hebrew Scriptures, from Genesis to Revelation, clearly define GOD's intention to purge pagan sun god worship from the land promised to Abraham—and then to eradicate it from the entire Earth. The Creator has determined the purpose of this physical, conscious experience we call "life." He states clearly and emphatically how He **does**, and, perhaps more apropos to our day and time, how He **does not** wish to be worshipped.

Abraham was seventy-five years old when he left Babylon for a land that he had never seen, taking his nephew Lot and both of their families with him. Upon entering the land, Lot separated himself from Abraham and joined a prosperous Canaanite culture that had developed on the fertile plain, which is now the Dead Sea Valley. Lot made his residence in the city of Sodom. The prophet Ezekiel said, "The sin of Sodom was pride, fullness of bread, and abundance of idleness. She did not strengthen the hand of the poor and needy. They were haughty, and committed abominations" (Ezekiel 16:49-50). If you want to know how to get on the bad side of the Almighty, search the Scriptures for what GOD calls "abomination."

ROOD-imentary Explanation

The word "abomination" is translated from the harshest words in the Hebrew language, *toavah* and *sheqets*, meaning "perverted, disgusting, repulsive, repugnant, putrid, and vile." The self-indulgent, promiscuous lifestyle of the inhabitants of Sodom became known as the sexual perversion identified in Scripture as sodomy, named after the city. Sodomy is commonly known today as "homosexuality."

Angelic Rescue

Abraham was forewarned that the sin of Sodom might have reached the point that Divine intervention was required. Two angels, appearing as normal men, left Abraham's tent to see what was transpiring in the city of Sodom. Upon arrival, the angels were hospitably welcomed into the home of Lot. But an aroused group of homosexual men demanded that Lot send these strangers out to them so that they could rape them. Lot refused, so they attacked him on his front porch. The angels pulled Lot to safety inside the house and smote the entire mob with blindness. The Scriptures record that the depraved mob wore themselves out as they groped the house looking for the door.

At sunrise the two angels took Lot, his wife, and two daughters by the hand, and dragged them away from the city and from their material possessions. When they were at a safe distance, fire and brimstone rained down from Heaven onto the city. Some scientists believe that this is when the 3,000-mile Great Rift Valley was formed: when the Earth's crust fractured and belched fire and brimstone into the Heavens. As the brimstone showered down upon the cities, Abraham saw the smoke of Sodom rise up in the distance. The sky turned as black as the ceiling of his goat-hair tent. He had been promised that if only ten righteous men could be found in that city, it would be spared GOD's righteous judgment. From the darkening sky, he knew that the quota had not been met. But until the smoke cleared, Abraham had no idea that Lot and his family had been saved from destruction.

In the middle of the sun-parched Israeli desert, the ashen remains of the city of Gomorrah still stand—covered with millions of chunks of brimstone.

So, Where Are Sodom, Gomorrah, Admah, and Zeboim?

In recent centuries, legend has developed that the four cities were submerged in the briny depths at the south end of the Dead Sea. Yet, five hundred years after the event, Moses recorded that nothing remained of the cities of the plain except for brimstone, salt and ashes, and nothing grows there (Deuteronomy 29:23).

During the first century of the Common Era, Shimon Kefa, commonly known as Simon Peter, spoke of the remains of the cities as if they were commonly known among the Jews of his day, still standing as visible examples of the righteous judgment of GOD (2 Peter 2:6). In the second century, the Jewish Priest and historian, Josephus, spoke of their remains still standing in the Judean desert.

The Dead Sea has continued to recede since the days that the Scriptures were penned. If they had been visible in the days of Josephus, there is no way that they could now be submerged. Archaeological expeditions have been generously funded to find Sodom and Gomorrah in places that are contrary to the record of the Hebrew Scriptures. After many looked in the wrong places and found nothing, the cities of the Plain were discovered exactly where the Scriptures indicate: along the western shore of the Salt Sea, in the Dead Sea Valley Plain.

Three thousand, nine hundred and ninety-four years after the destruction of those cities, I found myself sitting on the wall of Herod's veranda, studying the geometrical formations spreading northeast of the Roman encampments. Knowing that 90-degree angles rarely occur in nature, the symmetry of what appeared to be a walled enclave in the middle of a series of square and rectangular edifices compelled me to plot my path to its eastern entrance. A year earlier, I had studied photographs that were shot from this same wall atop Masada. They belonged to an amateur archaeologist who believed that the structures on the desert floor below me are the remains of the city of Gomorrah. I ventured to this precipice as a skeptic, but one who had to determine the truth.

Why Do We Not Question These Things?

I, along with the vast majority of Americans born since the early 1950s, was trained in a United States government public re-education center. The American public school system had been philosophically re-engineered to produce a generation of docile, taxable consumers who never question the political, religious, or economic systems into which they were born.

The original foundation of the American education system was to teach an accurate understanding of history from the Scriptures. If the populace can read the Scriptures, they can never be stripped of their GOD-given rights acknowledged in the founding documents of the Republic. But the new, reorganized education system controlled out of Washington D.C. derides the Hebrew Scriptures as a litany of fairy-tales. And if there is no GOD, then there is no moral right or wrong, and we, as all animals, are reduced to survival of the fittest, and if it feels good, do it. Sodom and Gomorrah's ruling monarchy promoted this same prosperity-driven "do what thou wilt" lifestyle.

The past few generations in America have been taught that this physical, conscious experience called "life" is just the result of millions of years of aberrant, chance mutations in a purely mechanical universe, and that there is no GOD. Evolution, the religion of the atheist, is the only religion that may be taught in the government re-education day camps. The goal of this religious re-education

What the government giveth, the government freely taketh away.

program is to produce a populace that does not believe that there is a GOD. But, why would the "New Deal" federal government go through all of the trouble of attempting to rewrite the laws of science in order to produce a generation of "global village" idiots? Because this tactic is simple and effective: If there is no GOD, there are neither GOD-given rights nor GOD-given responsibilities, which the "Unanimous Declaration of the thirteen united States of America" unashamedly affirms. If there are no inalienable rights delegated from the Creator to man—of which no pope, king, or governmental tyrant has the authority to deprive the citizen—then we are all but slaves to the government, which by default, becomes the giver of all rights. And, what the government *giveth*, the government freely *taketh* away.

America's educational bureaucracy has raised up a generation, which promulgates the lie that the Hebrew Scriptures are myth. State-endowed academic archaeologists look for biblical sites far from the locations specified in the Scriptures. Many lavishly funded archaeological expeditions in the land of Israel have turned up nothing after years of excavation. They exalt their intellect over the scriptural record and come up empty-handed year after year. They are actually funded **"to not find"** evidence, and then arrogantly pronounce that events recorded in the Scriptures are literary inventions. While being paid handsome wages to work the empty archaeological sites of their imaginations, they deride and condemn those who are actually finding artifacts at the very places the Hebrew Scriptures indicate. Since waking up to the fact that most of what I learned from governmental and ecclesiastical sources was grossly inaccurate or deliberately misrepresented, I set out to prove that which had been recently brought to my attention by a biblically literate archaeologist: namely that the remains of the cities of the Dead Sea Valley Plain still stand as visible examples of the righteous judgment of the Living GOD—just as Shimon Kefa (Simon Peter) prophesied concerning the end of the age.

I am holding in my hand a chunk of brimstone that had rained down from Heaven.

My Trek to Gomorrah to See the Wrath of GOD for Myself

From my elevated vantage point on Masada, I could see how easily this area could have eluded detection. What was once described as a beautiful valley, well watered like the Garden of the LORD, is now one of the most desolate, inhospitable destinations on the planet.

The last cable car descended Masada as I retrieved my backpack from a security locker at the base of the mountain. I filled a dozen plastic containers with cool water and puzzled them into my backpack. With 32 pounds of fresh water, a shovel, a tent, and a compass, I cinched the belt of my pack across my hips and followed the fading taillights of the last tourist bus down into the darkening valley. About a mile down the asphalt road, I quickly cut to the left and picked my way through the dry streambed of a rock-strewn wadi. The light of the full moon gave ample illumination as I pressed my way out of the sight of any passing patrols. My chest heaved painfully as I struggled up a crumbling 60-degree ascent, sinking to my ankles with every step into the dusty powder dampened by a rare desert rain. As I grabbed for a handhold to assist my shaking legs, what appeared to be rock crumbled like handfuls of moist cornstarch.

Reaching the crest, I panted on my knees to clear the racing stars before my eyes. There, under the light of the full moon of Marheshwan 15 (the eighth biblical month), I saw a pale yellow rock protruding from the surrounding matrix in front of me. My stomach queased as the rock broke open under the pressure of my thumb and forefinger. Posing the nugget to my nose, the unmistakable aroma of rotten eggs brought tears to my eyes—tears of thanksgiving that my expectation had not been disappointed. I was holding in my hands a chunk of brimstone that had rained down from Heaven, incinerating the city that I had just entered at the top of my climb.

Alone, under the starry sky of the Israeli desert, I knelt in the ashen remains of the buildings and wept. I had lived to see one of the witnesses that GOD preserved for the last days. I would return to America with a burning testimony that the record of the Hebrew Scriptures is true. The sulfur in my hands was a piece of reality that could shatter the make-believe world of religious indifference—a chunk of "the wrath of GOD." I was holding in my hands the raw material for a bomb that could shatter the dream world of atheism, a potential flame that could burn down the walls of socialist intellectual slavery. I was holding a testimony of GOD's desire and ability to save those who trust and obey Him. This was the treasure for which I had crossed land and sea.

For the next seven days, I camped at the foot of two identical elongated pyramids that mark the entrance to the ancient temple complex at Gomorrah. Before sunrise each day, I began collecting brimstone samples, retreating into the shade of an ashen crevasse during the heat of the mid-day sun and returning to work when the sun dipped behind Mount Masada. The fourth evening, I hauled my cache to the roadside and buried it. If I was discovered and my brimstone confiscated, I would still have access to a treasure large enough to fill a small suitcase. That evening I returned to camp much later than I was usually comfortable doing. The paw prints of desert lions near my campsite in the morning made me uneasy about traveling at night, so I always attempted to be in my tent with a full view of the surrounding area before dark. Lions prowl the deserted ruins at night in search of desert gazelle, and I am noticeably slower than a gazelle—especially while carrying bags full of fragile brimstone.

In the failing light, I followed the paths that gazelle had cut up and down the treacherous cliffs and valleys; I found that I could reasonably negotiate their well-worn routes. Cresting a ridge that led onto a plateau, I saw where the gazelle had pawed away the top layer of ash to expose a deep pocket of a white substance that I had not noticed before. Getting down into the pocket on my hands and knees, I pinched the odorless, snow-white substance onto my tongue. I found the remaining element of what Moses had described thousands of years ago: "Nothing remains of those cities except for brimstone, **salt**, and ashes, and nothing grows there."

These mineral salts brought back to remembrance a course in Nuclear, Biological and Chemical Warfare from my days in the Marine Corps. After the atomic bombs were dropped, ending World War II in the Pacific, U.S. military inspectors at Hiroshima found piles of white powder near

Digging up the salts.

the blast site. Analysis proved the powder to be the mineral salts of the incinerated individuals, who were vaporized in the fireball. All that were left were piles of salt. That discovery and the salt licks of Sodom and Gomorrah may answer the question: What became of Lot's wife? The Scriptures indicate that she turned back to the doomed city and became not a literal pillar, but a "pillar" as a Hebrew figure of speech—a "memorial" of salt. All that's left of her, and the entire population, are the mineral salts, which the desert gazelle now eat.

Brimstone and Asphalt: a Deadly Combination

The buildings, streets, and walkways throughout the land of Israel are constructed primarily of "Jerusalem Stone," a common and abundant calcium rock. The inhabitants of Sodom and Gomorrah would no doubt have taken advantage of this stone, the most available building material in the region, for the construction of their homes, palaces, and fortress walls—just as is done today. Biblical historians attribute Sodom and Gomorrah's overt wealth to the flourishing vegetation and to the commercial value of the asphalt pits found in this once lush valley. The open pits that dangerously dot the shoreline have, in ancient and modern times, swallowed entire military units.

As long as you keep moving, you are fine, but if you stop for a moment, you begin to sink into the bottomless pits of goop. Asphalt, oozing from deep in the Earth, turns wadis near the Dead Sea shore into surreal landscapes. The builders of the cities on this plain had access to an unlimited supply of asphalt with which to cement their buildings into indestructible fortresses—indestructible, that is, until burning brimstone rained from the sky, igniting the asphalt mortar and turning the city into a raging inferno.

Jerusalem stone (which is calcium rock) plus sulfur plus fire yields gypsum ash, and that is exactly what remains of these cities. Structures appear as rock formations from a distance, but those who venture out into the deserted, lion-prowled wasteland soon find their treks laborious, as they sink ankle deep into the gypsum ash. When this ash is subjected to flame, it does not even change color; it has already been completely consumed. Substances burned with sulfur can have a higher remaining ash weight than the original substance. That may explain, in part, how Sphinx and pyramid-shaped objects remain standing through the centuries. The layers of ash, twisted and warped by the intense heat, finally settle into a form that much resembles the original object. The minimal rainfall in this desert contributes

The builders of ancient cities had access to an unlimited supply of asphalt with which to cement their buildings into indestructible fortresses.

to the longevity of these structures—slowly compacting the layers of ash over millennia.

Why Not Look in Places Indicated in Hebrew Scriptures?

In Genesis 13:10 we read:

> *And Lot lifted up his eyes, and beheld all the plain of Jordan, that it was well watered every where, before the LORD destroyed Sodom and Gomorrah, even as the garden of the LORD ..."*

We also read in Genesis 14:1:

The kings of the land of Shinar made war with the kings of Sodom, Gomorrah, Admah, Zeboim, and Zoar. All of their armies were gathered together to fight in the valley of Sodom, which (after the destruction of those cities) is now called the Salt Sea.

The four cities that were destroyed by fire and brimstone are cited in Genesis 10:19 when it describes the borders of the land where the Canaanites settled after they left Babylon, following the confusion of the languages at the Tower of Babel. The borders of the Canaanites are as follows:

*... from Sidon, as thou comest to Gerar, unto Gaza; as thou goest, unto **Sodom**, and **Gomorrah**, and **Admah**, and **Zeboim**, even unto Lasha.*

The four cities could **only** form the *western* border of the Canaanites (*"as thou goest"*) if they were spread out along the Jordan River Valley, and not grouped together at the south end of what is now called the Dead Sea—as some modern archaeologist have proposed. But it appears that the bottom of the sea is the best place that one can look for these cities—and be certain **not** to find them. In 1 Samuel 13:16-18 we read:

... The Philistines camped at Mikmas, and raiding parties went out from the camp in three detachments: one turned toward Ophrah in the vicinity of Shual, another toward Beth Horon,

*and the third toward the border of the land
overlooking the Valley of Zeboim facing the desert.*

With the known locations of the Ophrah and Beth Horon, which are inhabited to this day, the location of the remains of Zeboim is easily confirmed as **north** of the Dead Sea, and is designated as: facing the desert, in the Great Rift Valley, east of Mikmas. When this ancient biblical map was followed, the ashen remain of Zeboim was found in the same condition as the city of Gomorrah.

How Certain is This Find?

Four locations, inclusive of Gomorrah, have yielded the same ashen features and the same remains of brimstone that we see in the city of Gomorrah. The brimstone found here is unique to this part of the Earth. Sulfur is a common element, but samples analyzed from different areas of the globe show that only crystalline sulfur reaches the purity of that found here in Gomorrah. Samples have been analyzed in laboratories in the U.S. and also in one of the most prestigious laboratories in the world, the Karolinska Institute in Stockholm, Sweden, which awards the Nobel Prize in the field of science. Critical analysis shows the sulfur found at Gomorrah to be 95.72 percent pure sulfur with three other trace metals, which could generate sufficient heat to melt even stainless steel.

The Smithsonian Institute in Washington D.C. maintains an exhaustive collection of natural sulphur compositions from around the world, but nothing that has been found on the rest of the planet has the characteristics of the brimstone found in these four locations along the ancient Canaanite border. The brimstone found at these four locations appears to be unique to the planet. According to Israeli geological scientists, these brimstone nuggets (*Gophrit* in Hebrew) are found *only* in these four locations in Israel.

Now, one can witness the increased frequency of tour buses that stop along the highway to Masada. From the comfort of their air-conditioned coaches, Israeli guides point at the tell-tale edifices in the distance as they relate the story of the ashen remains of Gomorrah, which still lie in the barren desert in the Dead Sea valley.

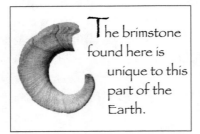

The brimstone found here is unique to this part of the Earth.

On our A ROOD Awakening! tours of Israel, our coach arrives at Gomorrah before sunrise, and everyone has a personal stash of brimstone before the sun rises high enough to force our evacuation to the oasis at Ein Gedi.

Demonstrating Heat and Discovering Mercy

Upon returning to Jerusalem, I found that my roommate, Joshua Cohen, had moved from the hostel where we had been staying. I went to the western wall of the Temple Mount to pray—I had to find Cohen, and I had no idea of where to begin looking for him.

Taking a leisurely route through the Jewish Quarter, I became entangled in the maze of streets in an unfamiliar area of the Old City. I heard a familiar voice coming from the basement of a darkened building as I passed. Backing up several steps, I called out, and Cohen answered with an enthusiastic shout. He and several mutual friends had moved and checked into the HaMalik hostel.

With no wasted time, I produced a chunk of brimstone and began relating my adventures since leaving for the desert a week earlier. Cohen had been apprised of the Gomorrah find a year earlier and was anxious to see the evidence. He had the brilliant idea of lighting a piece of the brimstone, and our friend Moshe immediately produced a book of matches. The nugget of sulfur immediately became engulfed in a purple flame as it turned into a black, oozing, bubbling mass that emitted a pungent stench.

Within moments, we began to choke and gag as the hot sulfur dioxide seared our lungs. A fearsome reality jolted my mind the moment that the sulfur hit my lungs. "This is deadly poison!" I choked out. "Clear the

"This is deadly poison!" I choked out. "Clear the building!"

building!" I scooped up the flaming brimstone with a stainless steel fork and headed for the door with the incredulous inhabitants of the hostel close behind. The cobblestone street was a perfect place to conclude the demonstration, and we held the bewildered pedestrian traffic at a safe distance until the brimstone burned out.

That was the last time I lit a piece of brimstone indoors. But, I did learn a valuable lesson: Being unable to breathe in the presence of the poisonous gasses emitted from the brimstone, the inhabitants of the cities had been rendered unconscious. They died relatively painless deaths before their bodies, and diseases, were incinerated by the ensuing inferno. Even in judgment, our Creator is merciful.

Getting My Treasure into the United States

A month later, I returned to the United States with my carry-on flight case filled to capacity with brimstone, salt, and ashes. I prayed for GOD's favor and protection, as I had no idea of how I might describe the contents of that case to get it through security. Israeli security did not open my bags, and my brimstone case passed through x-ray without raising an eyebrow. German security in Frankfurt passed me through without question, and it looked as though I was home free as I boarded my last plane for the States ... that was, until American customs ruled that the walking stick that I had hewn from a pruned Kidron Valley olive tree was an agricultural product. I was escorted to the "strip search" line, where my bags were completely rifled by the U.S. Department of Agriculture.

With one bag left to check, they found the prize of the day. "Look what we have here, gentlemen," the agent crowed, as he dramatically withdrew the sun-bleached skull of a desert gazelle that had been devoured by the lions of Gomorrah. It was a beautiful specimen that I was certain that my youngest daughter would treasure. They fairly understood when I told them the details of how I had procured it, but they insisted that if it is an endangered species, it must be confiscated and I could be charged with smuggling. The U.S. Department of Fish and Wildlife was called in on the case.

Hours passed as I prayed silently at "parade rest" in front of the inspection counter. During the wait, several intermediate inspectors listened to and evaluated my story concerning the skull.

Finally, the "grand inquisitor general" appeared with the books of knowledge, but he was also unable to come to a conclusion on the identity of the species of gazelle. He then explained that they must confiscate the skull and send it to a specialist. If it were found to be contraband, I would not be charged with smuggling because of my innocence in procuring it—if the experts couldn't identify the skull, then I couldn't be expected to know what it was either. If it turned out to be just an ordinary desert gazelle skull, it would be shipped to me at their expense.

He thanked me for my patience, and I bid them adieu as they passed me through without ever looking in the last suitcase—the one full of brimstone. I now had the world's largest privately held collection of brimstone on Planet Earth. The skull was returned to me "special delivery," and was in my daughter's hands within the month.

GOD Sets a Good and Bad Ensample

In Shimon Kefa's [Simon Peter's] second letter to the followers of Y'shua of Nazareth, known by many today as "Jesus," Kefa writes,

> GOD condemned the cities of Sodom and Gomorrah and turned them into ashes, making them an **ensample** to those that live ungodly lives ... (II Peter 2:6).

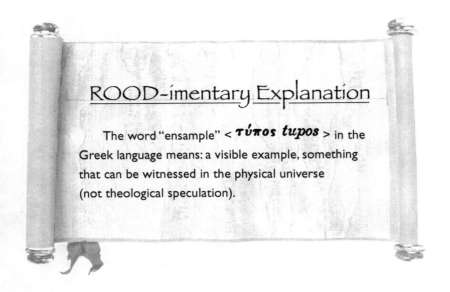

ROOD-imentary Explanation

The word "ensample" < τύπος *tupos* > in the Greek language means: a visible example, something that can be witnessed in the physical universe (not theological speculation).

Just as surely as the Almighty does not rain fire and brimstone down on every generation or city in which there is gross wickedness, He has left testimony on the Earth for these last days: GOD is the righteous judge, and if you decide to live an ungodly life, your judgment is just as sure as the judgment of Sodom and Gomorrah. The remains of Sodom and Gomorrah are also testimony to the righteous. Lot remained faithful in the midst of a sick, twisted, and perverse world. GOD delivered the righteous in the day of His judgment then, and He will deliver the just as He shakes the Earth in these last days.

The Nature of Judgment and Righteous Wrath

Many people have very pessimistic attitudes toward the judgment of GOD. When someone speaks of "GOD's judgment" on a nation, or of GOD judging the Earth, many perceive that judgment as a negative thing. Whether GOD's righteous judgment is negative or positive depends on whether you are *in* the wrong, or whether you *have been* wronged. When one gets his day in court, and righteous judgment is handed down from the bench, those who have been wronged celebrate—they have been vindicated and will be compensated for the evil they have suffered. Those who have wronged others are punished: recompensed for the evil that they have wrought.

GOD's judgment on Sodom brought relief to those who were shackled in dungeons until they were abused to death. It ended the rape and murder of other men who had entered into the city,

GOD's judgment on Sodom brought relief to those who were shackled in dungeons until they were abused to death.

expecting to conduct business and then return to their wives and children, only to be defiled mercilessly before being bludgeoned to death by their assailants. It ended child pornography and sex slave markets. It ended kidnapping and prostitution rings. It ended the murder of babies conceived in the free sex atmosphere of Sodom's singles' bars, church dating clubs, and the private studies of lawless clergy. Perhaps it ended the first syphilis and AIDS epidemics that could have wiped out the world before the age of modern medicine.

GOD is the righteous judge, and if you are living a righteous life, you yearn for the day that His righteous wrath is released upon the face of the Earth. As it is written in the

Psalms, "The righteous speak of His judgments all the day long ..." but, as I say, "His judgment is not pleasant table conversation in the house of the wicked." As Shimon Kefa said, "Even though we do not see GOD's hand of judgment overtly revealed against the wicked, do not deceive yourself into thinking that the Almighty is slack in His promise of judgment—He is not. He is longsuffering, not willing that any should perish" (2 Peter 3:9). He never judges without fair warning. Consider this visible example of brimstone, salt, and ash from the city of Gomorrah to be fair warning. The Seventh Millennium, the Sabbath Millennium, the Day, (or Millennium) of the LORD is at hand.

Just as Kefa had prophesied, the remains of the cities of Sodom and Gomorrah stand as an ensample, a visible witness in the last days that the Hebrew Scriptures are an accurate historical record of the land and people of which they speak. The ashen remains of those cities are testimony to those who decide to live an ungodly life. They remind us that the Judge, though longsuffering, will render a swift and terrible verdict to those who disobey His commandments and "do their own thing." This brimstone is also an aromatic reminder that the GOD of Abraham, Isaac, and Jacob is the **righteous** Judge, and that **He** will deliver the righteous in the coming Day of Judgment.

CHAPTER TWO

Willful Ignorance

The Acme of Foolishness

In the same breath that Peter speaks of the last days' testimony of the visible remains of Sodom and Gomorrah, in 2 Peter 3:4-5, he goes on to say:

> *Knowing this first, that there shall come in the last days **scoffers**, walking after their own lusts, And saying, Where is the promise of his coming? for since the fathers fell asleep, all things continue as they were from the beginning of the creation.*

Things Are About to Shake in Apocalyptic Proportions

When we read Peter's entire letter, we see that he is speaking by Divine Revelation. He says that the principle thing for those living in the last days to understand is that false ministers will rise up in the body of believers. These false ministers will be self-serving, personal kingdom-building religionists who will scoff at the reality of the promised personal return of the Messiah to rule the Earth. In the religious world, many pander to the crowd with, "Jesus could return before you take your next breath." It is impossible to change the course of your life in that short amount of time. But if people are faced with the possibility that they have a more precise number of years remaining in which to make their lives count, then that takes on a very challenging tone. You can do something constructive, and it probably isn't tearing down your current barn and building another one that will also be empty the majority of the week. The responsibilities of the last generation will be much different than the responsibilities of generations that have gone before. Things are about to shake in apocalyptic proportions. Life will not continue to flow gently down the dreamy stream of religion. Peter continues:

> *Of this they will be **willingly ignorant** ... GOD judged the world in the days of Noah and in the last days He will judge the world again.*

For one to be **willingly ignorant**, the facts must be available. As I travel the United States, sharing the archaeological finds that have come to light since the people of Israel began returning back to their Land, I am amazed by the indifference of the vast majority of those who identify themselves as "Christians." In the pseudo-scientific world of programmed atheism that permeates the modern educational system of America, it becomes important to present the myriad of irrefutable proofs of the creation origin of man, as well as the archaeological testimonies of the veracity of the Hebrew Scriptures. These proofs are effective tools in the hands of the educated believer. But tools are unnecessary for those who do not work. The modern Christian shows up one hour a week at the religious welfare administration building for milk and crackers. They have all of the tools they really need in life: a couch, a TV remote control, and a comfortable pew once a week. However, the Creator has preserved the greatest tools as a testimony of His power and authority. These tools are for His servants, not the pew-warming casual Christian or the uninterested innocent bystander.

Noah's Ark Has Been Found

How could someone be willfully ignorant concerning the shaking of the Earth in the time of Noah, unless sufficient evidence was found to prove that it actually transpired according to the record in the Bible? I suggest that even if Noah's Ark were found today, it would have little impact on modern Churchianity. In fact, unless the Noah's Ark was found by "their" denomination, the find would be practically irrelevant to the average Christian. But, like it or not, the Turkish Government has declared that the petrified remains of Noah's Ark have been found right where the Hebrew Scriptures indicated—in the mountains of Uratu in Northern Turkey.

In 1959, an American military pilot, surveying the mountains of Northern Turkey with stereo imaging photography, captured a giant boat-shaped object on film. A predominately military team from the United States undertook an expedition to the mountains of Ararat to investigate the anomaly. In typical military investigative fashion, they blew a hole in the structure with a charge of dynamite and then announced that it was "of no archaeological significance." One of the team members was Dr. Arthur Brandenberger and he was not convinced. He stated that there was not one member of the expedition who was qualified to assess the composition of the boat-shaped object. Years later another team returned to the site and secured samples of the rock-hard, boat-shaped structure. The rock contained high levels of organic carbon. Those rocks had, at one time, been alive. They were, in fact, petrified wood. Carbon 14 dating, which can only be used to test once-living matter, confirmed that the structure was approximately 5,000 years old—which is unusually accurate for Carbon 14 dating!

Since the image of the boat-shaped object appeared on the cover of *Life* magazine in 1960, Ron Wyatt, a medical professional, could not shake the conviction that these were the petrified remains of Noah's Ark. After nearly two decades of testing the terrain and his theories against the biblical record, Ron and his two sons made the journey to northern Turkey to investigate the site. He was given permission by the Turkish government to take measurements and obtain samples for testing.

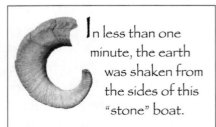

In less than one minute, the earth was shaken from the sides of this "stone" boat.

The ancillary evidence was building a strong case, but in 1978 an earthquake in Northern Turkey revealed even more. The earthquake fault went right down the middle of the boat-shaped object. In less than one minute, the earth was shaken from the sides of this "stone" boat. The surrounding matrix of earth dropped away, exposing 30 to 50 feet of the sides of the Ark around its entire perimeter. The hand of the Almighty excavated the Ark in one minute, more than archaeologists could have done in 100 hundred years with modern equipment. Hundreds of running feet of horizontal deck support timbers and rib timbers were preserved in a petrified state. The opened earthquake fissure allowed the collection of plant fibers, animal hair, and copious amounts of petrified animal dung from deep within the bowels of the ship. The ship could now be accurately measured to exactly 500 "Divine" or "Royal Egyptian" cubits of exactly 20.62 inches in length, just as Moses was taught how to measure in the court of Pharaoh. The depth and width of the boat are also consistent with the biblical record, allowing for the natural splaying of a decaying wooden ship.

After years of work with ship salvage experts, scientists from Los Alamos labs, and oil field researchers with subsurface interface radar equipment, and after analyzing the scriptural record and the remaining cultural clues, Wyatt presented his findings to the Turkish government. They turned to one of the most recognized authorities on antiquities in the world, Ekrem Urkegal, famous for his discovery of the ancient Hittite civilization, which for centuries had eluded archaeologists. After pouring over the data provided by Wyatt and his colleagues, as well as analyzing other data from the scientific community, Urkegal's team concluded their assessment in their report to the Turkish government, "This is a boat; it is an ancient boat; and it must be preserved."

Although Wyatt and Urkegal would both readily admit that no petrified plaque has been found which bears the inscription "Noah's Ark—3000 BC," the Turkish government was confident in the scientific evidence and constructed a visitors' center and a multi-million dollar, four-lane highway to bring visitors to the site. The regional tourist maps point the way to "Nuhan Gimesi" (Noah's Big Boat), and road

The Turkish Government has declared that the petrified remains of Noah's Ark have been found right where the Hebrew Scriptures indicated—in the mountains of Uratu in Northern Turkey.

signs boldly display the distance to the petrified Ark and to the international visitors' center that overlooks the Ark. Even at that, pulpit potatoes continue to scoff.

CNN briefly covered some of the events surrounding the discovery of Noah's Ark when a research expedition consisting of Wyatt, Rives, Wilson, and Roberts were captured by Kurdish rebels and forced at gunpoint through the mountains of Ararat for 21 days. Forty-five hundred Turkish troops pursued the Kurds, burning down forests and sniping at the rearguard of the rebel forces. After two weeks, the U.S. State Department gave up hope of bringing the Americans back alive. They packed up their choppers and flew home; no one had ever returned alive after being captured by the Kurds. But when all hope was lost, the group made a daring escape during transport to what may have been their executions. Thousands of prayers were answered by their miraculous deliverance.

Even ABC's news program *20/20* had a short special on the Noah's Ark find. But during the time that the real Ark story was starting to receive the recognition that would force the eyes of the world open, CBS news aired a deliberate farce that bolstered the myth that Noah's Ark is in the Ohura Gorge on Mount Ararat itself.

Mount Ararat is a 17,000-foot post-flood volcano that did not exist in the time of Noah and is not mentioned in the biblical record. The Ohura Gorge was formed when the side of Mount Ararat blew out in a volcanic eruption in the early 1800s. The pseudo-scientific documentary that CBS aired enlisted professional actors and contrived false evidence to construct an intentional hoax. When called on the incident, CBS excused their misleading "documentary" with the explanation that their program was just an "entertainment special" and that they are not required to be accurate, truthful, or to even inform their audience that they have been deliberately deceived.

I can understand why the mainstream media turn a blind eye to this discovery—they are committed to upholding the socialist state religion of Evolution. Scientific realities that would support the biblical perspective are counterproductive to the advancement of the new religion of state. But why have we not heard more about the discovery of the Noah's Ark in the Christian circles in America? Many Europeans go to the site each year, but where are American Christians vacationing? My experience has led me to the realization that unless one's own particular denomination found Noah's Ark, the find has no validity. Certainly, if GOD were going to do anything so magnanimous as revealing Noah's Ark, He would do it through the Southern Baptist Convention—or the Episcopalians—or the Assemblies of GOD—or the "holy" Roman Catholic empire—or whatever cult to which one ascribes. Peter said it best:

> *Of this they will be willingly ignorant ... GOD judged the world in the days of Noah, and in the last days He will judge the world again.*

When, Not If, GOD Shakes Things Up

To be willingly ignorant indicates that there must be substantial evidence to the truth, but that religious leaders in the last days will have an agenda that diverges from GOD's plan, causing them to turn a blind eye to reality. They will specialize in keeping their flocks in the dark, feeding them the diet of a mushroom in order to realize their own dreams of peace, comfort, and ecclesiastical immortality. In the days of Noah, GOD shook the foundations of the Earth, but this next time, He is going to shake not only the Earth, but the Heavens, as well. (Isaiah 13:13, Joel 3:16, Haggai 2:6, 21) Everything that can be shaken is about to be shaken. The only things that are going to be left standing are those things that are grounded and founded on rock. Make no mistake. It is GOD who is going to do the shaking. Y'shua said, "**When** the wind blows, and **when** the floods come." He did not say, "**If.**" Y'shua was prophesying about the time that the Hebrew prophets refer to as "the time of Jacob's trouble." That is the time in which GOD has promised that He is going to shake things up, and Peter writes very pointedly concerning the time of this shaking—that we are not to be ignorant of this one thing, that "one day is with the LORD as a thousand years, and a millennium as one day" (2 Peter 3:8).

So, **when** will GOD shake things up? The Hebrew understanding of this scripture in 2 Peter is that **when** the seventh or the Sabbath millennium begins, the shaking of the Earth will transpire. That period of time will be "the day" or "the millennium" of the LORD.

CHAPTER THREE

Learning to Tell Time Biblically

Peter insists that there is one thing about which we, the aware Believers, are absolutely **not** to be ignorant, and that is the issue concerning the day of the LORD when the shaking of the Earth begins. Shimon was speaking about the very thing that the rabbis have taught for thousands of years: "In that GOD created the Heavens and the Earth in six days, and on the seventh day He rested. Man will have his time of rule on the Earth for 6,000 years, and the Messiah will reign in the Seventh or the Sabbath millennium, the Day, or the Millennium of the LORD."

In the second century book named after its author, Barnabas stated that just as GOD created the Heaven and the Earth in six days, and the seventh day He rested, the Messiah would reign in the Seventh or Sabbath Millennium, the Day, or the Millennium of the LORD. This is suggested throughout the Hebrew Scriptures.

Michael Rood holding the Torah—a scroll of the five books of Moses.

The first century Jewish followers of the Messiah were under no delusion that the Messiah could return "at any moment." That modern fallacy is a Western Gentile Christian fabrication that has been extrapolated out of Greek exegetical exercises rather than from the plain text of the Scriptures. According to Peter, we are not to be ignorant of the mathematical testimony that GOD has reserved for us in the last days. That testimony reads: "A day with the LORD is as a thousand years, and a thousand years, is as a day."

The Christian world is not taught basic biblical math in church. Most churchgoers, for example, have been brought up believing that the crucifixion of Messiah took place on Good Friday afternoon, and that He left the tomb before sunrise on Easter Sunday. However, the Messiah himself said that there was going to be only **one** sign given to a wicked and adulterous generation, and that is the sign of the prophet Jonah. "As Jonah was three days and nights in the whale's belly, so shall the son of man be **three** days and **three** nights in the heart of the Earth" (Matthew 12:40).

There is not one ecclesiastical mathematician who can possibly get three days and three nights out of the religious world's reckoning of Good Friday to Easter Sunday as the time frame for the death and resurrection of Y'shua. If we, by our Babylonian reckoning of time and by our Gentile interpretation of the Hebrew Scriptures, destroy the only sign given to us, there is little hope that we would ever be able to do the advanced mathematical calculations to which Peter alludes. Our greatest theologians cannot even count to three! Our generation is obviously the twisted and perverse generation to which Y'shua refers!

How Do We Measure Time?

Adam's first year was the year 1, and the first millennium was the year 1 through the year 1000. The second millennium began in the year 1001 and went through the year 2000. The third millennium began in the year 2001 and went through the year 3000. When we reach the year 6001, we will have arrived at the Seventh, or Sabbath Millennium, the Day, or the Millennium of the LORD. The year 6001 will also be the 120th jubilee year from the time of creation. We see that equation in the book of Genesis when GOD spoke to Adam and said,

> In **the day** you eat thereof (of the tree of the knowledge of good and evil) thou shalt surely die (Genesis 2:17).

But, the Scriptures also tell us that Adam lived for 930 years after his transgression. How do we reconcile that apparent contradiction? Adam was created to live forever, but he died in **the day**, or **the millennium** in which he was created. Even though Methuselah came close at a life span of 969 years, no one has ever lived past **day one**, or the **first millennium** of his or her existence. A day with the LORD is as a thousand years; a thousand years are as a day.

Does Anybody Really Know What Time It Is?

According to the modern Jewish calendar, in September of the Gregorian year 2000, we entered the Jewish year 5761. The year 5761 would indicate that we were, at the time, at least 240 years away from the year 6001, the beginning of the Seventh, or the Sabbath Millennium. However, Jewish scholars do not dispute the fact that many years have been subtracted from the elapsed time reckoning since creation. There is a consensus among rabbinic and Christian scholars alike that many years were subtracted. The question is, "How many years?" It was the noted Jewish rabbi, Shimon Schwab, who stated that he could prove that there are at least 165 years missing from the total elapsed time calendar, and perhaps many more.

So, the question remains: What year is it now? Among the Western Gentile, or Christian chronologists, there are few who would argue with these following statements: The creation of Adam was *around* the year 4000 BCE (Before the Common "Error"—in calculating the birth of Y'shua). We are now, *around* the year 2000 of the Common "Error." Any second grade student would be able to add this together and see that 4000 BCE plus 2000 CE would bring us to *around* the year 6000 from creation. But in the Western world, we are not taught the biblical reckoning of time, and so Christians find themselves seriously hampered in their understanding of the Hebrew Scriptures and unable to accurately calculate the beginning of the Day or the Millennium of the LORD.

In the middle of the second century, the leader of the Pharisees, Rabbi Akiva, deliberately subtracted more than 200 "years in captivity" from the elapsed time calendar in order to get the birth year of his personal choice of messiah, Simon bar Kochba to fit with the rabbinic understanding that the Messiah would arrive in the fourth millennium from creation. Even though the bar Kochba revolt ended with the death of Rabbi Akiva and his false messiah, the calendar was never again rectified with the actual year from creation. Hence, rabbinic tradition continued to obscure the truth from the general masses.

The *Book of Genealogies*, which was written by Ezra upon his return from Babylon, was hidden several centuries ago by Jewish scholars. This *Book of Genealogies* contains chronological information, which allowed ancient scholars to determine the exact year from creation. Actually, however, we may not be lost in time after all. Due to a public declaration the week of March 26, 2001, it is suspected by some that the *Book of Genealogies* has again surfaced in the land of Israel. Evidence from several sources suggests that the Millennium of the LORD may have already begun.

Actually, however, we may not be lost in time after all.

The Millennium of the LORD Has Begun

At sundown on March 26, 2001, the new moon appeared over the city of Jerusalem. According to the ancient reckoning of time as stipulated in the Scripture, it was the beginning of the month. On the day before the new moon sighting, the barley on the Temple Mount was declared to be "aviv." According to the ancient reckoning, this was the month of the Aviv barley, the beginning of the biblical year.

Twice during this week of March 26, 2001, a large contingency of both Sephardi and Ashkenazi rabbis met at the western wall of the ancient Temple Mount in Jerusalem to make a unanimous declaration: "The time of Jacob's trouble has **now** begun!" (It is significant that these two groups of rabbis were able to agree on this issue; they, in fact, disagree on so many things, that two different versions of the same religious books are published to cater to each point of view.) It was also during this week that our calendar research team back in America determined that the Astronomically and Agriculturally Corrected Biblical Hebrew Calendar (AACBHC) had reached the date of Aviv 1, 6001. The Day

"The time of Jacob's trouble has now begun!"

or the Millennium of the LORD had begun. Seven months later, on Tishri 10—on Yom Kippur, the 120th Jubilee from creation began. Would we begin to see the time of trouble that will ultimately deliver all of the land from the Euphrates River to the River Nile into the hands of those to whom it is promised?

We are living in GOD's universe. The world in which we live is synchronized to GOD's calendar and GOD's time clock. Whether we know about it or not is inconsequential, because GOD does not spin the universe around the things we do or do not understand. In the Western world, we have forsaken GOD's reckoning of time, which is clearly outlined in the Hebrew Scriptures. We have inherited a pagan reckoning of time, completely out of touch with reality and contrary to GOD's reckoning. It is as if the hands have been broken from the face of the clock. We don't know what time it is. But GOD knows what time it is; He has a plan that was first declared in the book of Genesis, and He made a promise to the people of Israel, which will not go unfulfilled.

We will not see the immediate reign of Messiah upon the Earth or His return in the clouds at the beginning of the Seventh, or Sabbath Millennium. First, we will see the intermediate fulfillment of the Fall Feasts of the LORD and the gathering of the twelve tribes to the land of their full inheritance. We will see the sons of Israel finally take possession of all of the land from the Euphrates to the Nile, which was promised to Abraham's descendants through his son Isaac. We will see Islam rise and fall. Mankind will bring itself to the brink of destruction. The hand of the Almighty will be revealed in the Seventh Millennium, the Day or Millennium of the LORD. Only *then* will we see the glorious coming of the Son of GOD who will gather His saints and rule the Earth with a just and unbending rod. Now is the time to get ready for the tumultuous time ahead.

I will see you when the smoke clears ...

BOOK TWO

Truth vs. Tradition:
The Heavyweight
Battle of the Ages

CHAPTER ONE

Truth and Tradition

Traditions can blind us from the truth and cause us to wander for an entire lifetime in the myopic fog of man-made religious systems. Many of the traditions of the Western Gentile Christian church are merely adapted pagan worship rituals inherited from our ancestors. They were forced to compromise with the Roman Emperor Constantine or lose their lives for refusing to bow. Most of these traditions were imported directly from Babylon. In fact, there is not a single religion practiced upon the face of the Earth today that has not been polluted by Nimrod's rebellion against the one true GOD.

The Hebrew Scriptures expose the perverted traditions of man-made religions and offer reality to those who hunger and thirst for truth. Shaul—commonly know as the apostle Paul, a first century rabbi, Pharisee, and, finally, a follower of Y'shua of Nazareth—wrote that we should not be misled by traditions and commandments of men (Colossians 2:22) but rather rely upon the tested and proven source of truth— the Torah, the five books of Moses. The children of Israel camped at Mount Sinai for an entire year as Moses passed on the instructions from the Creator. These instructions, called "Torah" in Hebrew, taught us how to govern ourselves, and throw off the shackles of manmade religious, political, and economic systems. Y'shua, or as many know him by his Gentile nickname, "Jesus," warned His followers that traditions promulgated by religious leaders are like leaven or yeast, which once mingled with dough, cannot be removed. Without the Torah of GOD, it is impossible to separate the traditions of men from the rules of the Almighty.

Jeremiah said that in the last days, the Gentiles would come to the sons of Israel and cry out in repentance, "Surely our fathers have inherited lies ..." (Jeremiah 16:19). If our

ROOD-imentary Explanation

The English word "tradition" is derived from the Latin *tradiere*, which means, "to lay into the hands of another." When someone lays something into your hands, you expect the intention of the gift to be good. But it is the responsibility of the recipient to inspect the gift. Traditions can be good or evil; the recipient must carefully inspect that which is laid into his hands.

fathers have inherited lies, what they pass on to us does not magically become "the truth" by virtue of their sincerity. Traditions are given to us in innocence and accepted in ignorance. We are like the blind following the blind. Those who are **leading** us might not have any intention of **misleading** us, but they are nonetheless blind, and we will both certainly fall into a ditch unless we have our eyes opened to the truth.

But, what is truth? Truth is reality—that which *is*. Truth is reality whether one believes it or not. One can believe **a lie** his entire life, but it will never change into **reality** to suit his belief system. If we are to live the truth, we must be willing to constantly challenge the traditions and teachings that we have inherited from our parents and religious systems, as well as our own comfortable patterns of thinking.

A Traditional Myth About Daniel

There is a reason for **every** word in the Scriptures. There is purpose underlying what is said, how it is said, when it is said, and to whom it is said. I was an adult before I questioned the picture in my mind of Daniel as a young boy, standing safely in the lion's den. Once that picture was embedded, I had no reason to question its validity. Years later, however, a new picture developed from the Scriptures: an old Daniel, 80ish, who had been a ruler of Babylon under Nebuchadnezzar, Belshazzar, and now Darius, who was tricked into having his vice-president Daniel executed.

Daniel and his Jewish companions, Azriyah, Haniniyah and Misha'el, were reared in Jerusalem and taught the Torah from their youth. When they were carried away as captives into Babylon, they were renamed Belteshazzar,

Shadrack, Meshech and Abed-nego, made eunuchs, and trained for service in the court of King Nebuchadnezzar (Daniel 1:1-7). Daniel accurately interpreted one of the King's troubling dreams and was meritoriously promoted to Prime Minister, which made him an extremely wealthy young man. The Scriptures specifically state that Daniel was multiplied in wealth twice more: during the reigns of Belshazzar and again under Darius the Mede. Daniel was one of the richest men in the kingdom. For more than 60 years, Daniel was in charge of the "Chaldeans," a group of highly trained astronomers and intellectuals, among whom were many Judean captives. During the course of his life, Daniel received many dreams and visions about kingdoms to come ... and the end of the age.

Near the end of his life, he was visited by the Archangel Gavriel and given very exact timing concerning the coming of the Messiah, but he was instructed to seal up some of the information. Apparently it was for him, and him alone, to understand and act upon. Daniel died in Babylon, a eunuch with no heir to whom he could leave his wealth, but there is little doubt that he would have made careful plans for the distribution of his vast treasure.

When we carefully consider the Scriptures and historical records of the time period, we see a very compelling picture develop. Many of the Jews, especially those in positions of responsibility, stayed behind in Babylon after the captivity had ended—the most notable being Mordechai and his niece Haddasa (also known as Queen Esther, who became the bride of the King). Daniel would have naturally delegated the execution of his will to his most trusted companions, the

Jewish Chaldean astronomers, whom he had trained, and who remained behind in Babylon.

But what became of Daniel's estate? It would be nearly 500 years before any hint of Daniel's treasure reappears in the pages of the Scriptures.

A Traditional Myth About the Nativity

Ask the man on the street, "How many wise men came to present gifts to Jesus, where did they find Him, and how was He dressed?" As you already know, the common answer is, "**Three** wise men found Jesus wrapped in **swaddling clothes** lying in a **manger.**" That, however, is not the testimony of the Scriptures. We read in the King James Version of Matthew's account that an undesignated number of wise men [in the Greek, *magi*, the common term for Chaldean astronomers] came to the **house** where they found the **young child**, Y'shua, living with his mother Miriam and step-father and Yoseph.

In the Gospel of Luke we read that **only** the **shepherds** arrived at the manger (Matthew 2:11, Luke 2:8-20).

It's absurd to suggest that a lonesome trio laden with treasure crossed the torrid sands of the desert without the protection of a large armed caravan. They would not have been "wise men," but fools, to have ventured unaccompanied into the desert. These magi were the descendants of Jewish Chaldean astronomers, who were entrusted with Daniel's treasure.

Following Daniel's instruction, the astronomers watched the skies for more than 500 years, awaiting the Great Sign in the Heavens that finally occurred on Tishri 1, at the end of the fourth millennium (Revelation 12:1-5). The constellation Bethula [Hebrew], the Virgin (*Virgo* [Latin]) was clothed with the setting sun at the time that the first sliver of the new moon appeared beneath her feet. In the twelve stars above her head, the planet Ha Tzadek—the righteous (*Jupiter* [pagan])—came into conjunction with the star Ha Maleck, the king star (*Regulis* [Latin]) that is between the feet of the constellation of Ariel [Hebrew] (*Leo* [Latin]) the Lion of Judah.

On the first day of the month of Tishri, on Yom Teruah— the Day of Trumpets—this one-time celestial alignment announced the upcoming birth of the Maleck-Tzadek, the righteous King of kings, the Lion of the tribe of Judah, who was to rule all nations with a rod of iron. Daniel had made provision for the Messiah and instructed the Chaldeans concerning the great sign in the heavens that would announce His birth.

Now, 500 years later, the executors of Daniel's will brought their treasure-laden caravan into the city gates of Jerusalem with the proclamation, "We have come to worship Him who is born the King of the Jews." Herod sent them to the neighboring village of Beit Lechem, where the prophet Micah said the Mashiach would be born (Micah 5:2).

Before Herod sent the Chaldean astronomers to Beit Lechem, he took private counsel with them, asking them

ROOD-imentary Explanation

Y'shua was actually born on the first day of the Feast of Tabernacles, the fifteenth day of the seventh month on the biblical calendar, which always occurs in autumn. His birth was an intermediate fulfillment of the Feast of Sukkot [or "Mangers," in Hebrew]. Yoseph was required to live in a sukkah, or tabernacle, during the entire 7-day feast. Miriam, his pregnant wife, was not required to live in the sukkah, but the Bethlehem Bed and Breakfast was completely booked, so she joined her husband in the sukkah on the first day of the Feast of Sukkot, and delivered her firstborn son there ... in the sukkah. That is the moment when "the Word was made flesh and sukkoted [or tabernacled] among us." In the King James Version of the Bible, tabernacled was translated as "dwelt" among us (John 1:14).

to return to him with information concerning the child's whereabouts. After the Chaldeans delivered Daniel's treasure to the Messiah, they were warned in a vision to secretly depart from Israel. Herod became furious that the astronomers had ignored his request, so he ordered that all of the male children throughout the hill country of Beit Lechem should be killed— all those who were "two years old and under according to the time which he had diligently inquired of the wise men" (Matthew 2:16). But by this time, Yoseph and Miriam and the young child, Y'shua, were well on their way to Egypt. The very night the Chaldean astronomers had delivered Daniel's treasure, Yoseph was commanded in a vision to take the child and his mother, and flee into Egypt.

Think about it: Yoseph was so impoverished that he could only afford the poor man's sacrifice of two pigeons at the child's dedication, which occurred 40 days after his birth. He was not yet in possession of any gold, frankincense, *or*

The one-time celestial alignment.

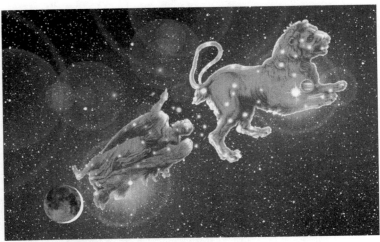

myrrh (Luke 2:22-24)! But, on the very night that Yoseph and his family had to escape into Egypt, the provision for their flight and sustenance arrived by special courier. The provision had been made 500 years earlier and was prepared for the very moment it was needed. The Almighty is the master of drama—when there appears to be no hope, His salvation is revealed at last!

Truth is always more exciting than fictitious traditions and fairy tales based on ignorance of the Scriptures. Leave your Western Gentile mentality behind as we explore the New Testament Scriptures from a Jewish or Hebrew perspective. This is the paradigm shift for which you have been waiting an entire lifetime!

Sweet Little Baby Tammuz

In the book of Ezekiel we read how an angel exposed the religious perversions that were being covertly conducted in the Temple.

> *The angel brought me to the gate of the house of the LORD and I beheld—women weeping for Tammuz. Then said he unto me, thou shalt see greater abominations. And he brought me into the inner court where about twenty-five men had their backs toward the Temple, and they faced the east and worshipped the sun (Ezekiel 8:14-16).*

Worship of the sun and of Tammuz started in ancient Babylon. Nimrod built a city as the epicenter of his world government. It was there in Babylon that Nimrod was worshipped as "god." He bore totalitarian rule over the people, reducing them to slaves in his political, economic, and religious systems. According to ancient Jewish tradition, it was Noah's righteous, eldest son Shem who slew Nimrod and scattered his body parts throughout the land of Shinar.

That should have effectively ended the worship of Nimrod, but his devoted followers erected a tower that reached into the heavens—a huge obelisk just like the ones we see in Washington D.C., Heliopolis (Egypt), Rome, London, Paris, New York City, and around the globe. These obelisks are images of the uncircumcised penis of Nimrod, the father of Babylonian sun god worship. The Creator calls this obelisk **"the image of jealousy"** and an **"abomination."** A previously broken down ancient Roman obelisk was re-erected in Israel in the summer of 2001. Coincidently, a homosexual perversion pride parade in Tel Aviv seemingly inaugurated its erection ... and in the month of Tammuz, no less!

Nimrod's widow, Beltis (also known as Semiramus), would not willingly let the kingdom slip through her fingers when her husband was killed. She proclaimed that Nimrod did not die, but that he had ascended into the heavens and was now the sun god. He later impregnated her with the rays of the sun. (At least, that was his widow's excuse.) She delivered that illegitimate child on the day of **the rebirth of the sun,** the Winter Solstice ... which, on the ancient Babylonian calendar (before the procession of the equinoxes), fell on

December 25th—the day that Nimrod, the sun god, was reborn as Tammuz.

The Significance of December 25

The December 25th birthdate of Tammuz, the Babylonian sun god, comes as a shock to some in the West, but is common knowledge among Jewish scholars and historians. The Jews were taken captive into Babylon for their disobedience concerning sun worship, even though they staunchly maintained, "That's not what 'Tammuz's birthday' means to us."

They had also been captives in Egypt, where they took on the worship of Ra, the Egyptian sun god who was born on ... December 25th.

In 168 BC, the Syrian/Greek General Antiochus Epiphanes occupied Jerusalem and set up a statue of Zeus in the Temple and proclaimed that Zeus was god ... on Zeus' birthday, December 25th.

When Rome conquered Persia, the Roman Army adopted the worship of Mithra, the Persian version of Babylonian Tammuz. The symbol of Mithra was the same as the symbol of Tammuz: the Babylonian *Tau*, or "cross." When Rome conquered Jerusalem, they hung Jewish patriots on the cross of Mithra as sacrifices to the Roman sun god who was born on ... you guessed it ... December 25th.

The confusion of languages at the Tower of Babel scattered the heathen into the far corners of the Earth and confused the names of their gods, but the rituals of worship remained much the same wherever they went. Many significant historical events concerning pagan worship occurred on December 25th; but of this one thing I can absolutely assure you—Y'shua of Nazareth was *not* born on ... December 25th.

But who was? Little baby Tammuz—the "reincarnated" Nimrod.

Forty Days of Weeping for Tammuz

Tammuz, so the story goes, was gored to death by a wild boar in a hunting accident when he was 40 years old. Hence, 40 days of weeping for Tammuz was instituted: one day for each year of his life. During that time, sun god worshipers would deny themselves a pleasure in this life, for the sake of Tammuz' pleasure in the afterlife.

Sound familiar? It gets better.

Easter Reconsidered

When Nimrod's wife, Tammuz's mother, died many years later, the exalted "Queen of Heaven" was sent back to earth by the gods on the first S-U-N day after the Vernal Equinox. She arrived in a giant egg, which landed in the Euphrates River and broke open to allow her to emerge, reincarnated as the bare breasted goddess of fertility and sexual desire. Her new name? Ishtar— Easter. To proclaim her divinity, Easter changed a bird into an egg-laying rabbit. On the western slope of the Hinnom valley in Jerusalem, in the dingy depths of the Canaanite caves designated for the worship of Easter and her son Tammuz, the priests of Easter would impregnate virgins on the altar of Easter at the Easter sunrise service. One year later the priests would sacrifice those three-month old infants on the same altar, and dye Easter eggs in the blood of those sacrificed babies. To this very day, one denomination allows their Easter eggs to be dyed only one color: **blood red!** When you ask them why, they have no idea how the tradition started or what it rehearses ... but now **you** know!

Easter Sun day (the day set aside for sun god worship) is the day that concludes the 40 days of weeping for Tammuz—called by many "Lent." From the time of its inception in Nimrod's Babylon until this very day, this 40-day pagan festival climaxes as the sun god worshippers kill "the wild boar that killed Tammuz" and eat "ham" after the Easter sunrise orgy and child sacrifice service. There is one day that I can assure you that Y'shua did **not** rise from the grave ... Easter sun day! And He **never** participated in "Lent!" WWJD? He would never, ever celebrate "Easter!"

Frequently, Easter and Passover are an entire month apart. Why? They represent the worship of two different gods. Easter is celebrated according to a pagan sun calendar developed in Babylon in accordance with the worship of Nimrod. Passover is celebrated according to the observance of the biblical new moon and ripening of the barley in the land of Israel. Y'shua kept the Feast of Passover. All of the rehearsals that were embedded in that feast were fulfilled the year of His resurrection. On the other hand, Easter is the rehearsal of child sacrifice and fertility rites of pagan sun god worshippers.

Make Your Choices Carefully!

Which celebration should you keep? It depends entirely upon which GOD you serve; it's your choice. Now you understand why the Holy One instructed us, "Do not learn the way of the Heathen and how they worship their gods, and then do the same to me – it is an abomination."

Christmas and Easter are **not** celebrations of the birth and resurrection of Y'shua of Nazareth, but the continuation of child sacrifice festivals that were **hatched** in Babylon two thousand years before His birth!

We all recognize that the pagan calendar, which has been adopted by the Christian world, names every day of the week and nearly every month of the year after a pagan god or fallen angel. But many are surprised to note that the fourth month on the modern Jewish calendar is named after the pagan god Tammuz, in direct violation of the Torah, which states, "Thou shalt not allow the names of other gods to come out of your mouth" (Exodus 23:12-14). I only speak the names of pagan gods for the same reason that the prophets of Israel spoke their names: to expose the perverted traditions that we have inherited from our disobedient ancestors.

CHAPTER TWO

Coming Out of Babylon

The Almighty called Abraham to come out of Babylon by crossing over the Euphrates River and entering into a place where his offspring would be given a parcel of land "flowing with milk and honey," and a job to do. Abraham's descendants were to purge the land of every last vestige of pagan sun god worship, and then they were to be YHWH's priests to the entire Earth. They were to be a nation of prophets who would make known the ways of the true GOD and call all nations to repentance. Israel was not obedient to the command to cleanse the land of paganism, but rather, they adopted the practices of the heathen.

For this rebellion, the ten northern tribes of Israel were spiritually blinded and scattered among the heathen until the time that their chastisement would be fulfilled—just as was prophesied by Moses and Ezekiel. The southern tribes in Judea were taken into Babylon because of their disobedience, and then later scattered throughout the earth by Rome until such time as they became a nation in *one day*, just as was prophesied by Moses, Isaiah, and Jeremiah. That *one day* occurred on May 15, 1948—the day when the modern State of Israel was born.

When You Know the Truth

Religious schemes have been fabricated by the twisted mind of man that have nothing to do with how GOD desires to be worshipped. Pop Christian culture adorns itself with the latest hip Jesus apparel and jewelry that asks, "What Would Jesus Do?"... but seldom opens the Scriptures to find out! Y'shua **found** the place where it was written, **said** what was written, and **did** what was written. He did not make up His own theology as He went along. He **always** obeyed the Torah and said that the Father seeks those who would worship Him in Spirit and in the truth that was written in stone over 3,500 years ago (John 4:21-26). When we are ignorant of His instructions, we naturally slip back into Babylonian sun god worship practices while we say we are doing them for Him. (Israel expressed the same overt disobedience and ignorance of GOD's ways when they built a golden calf and proclaimed, "Tomorrow is a feast to the LORD.")

Occasionally I hear the emotionally charged defense, "That is not what Christmas and Easter mean to me!" But I really don't care what it means to you. I don't worship you! The Almighty says that it is an **abomination** to **Him**. The Torah reminds us, "Do not learn the way of the heathen, how they worship and serve their gods, and then do the same and say that you are doing it for me, it is an abomination" (Deuteronomy 12:30-31). Just as the Almighty told Abraham in Genesis, He also, in the book of Revelation, tells those living at the end of the age to "come out of Babylon."

Studying Y'shua From a Jewish Perspective

In the following chapters of this book we will be exploring the Hebrew Scriptures—both Testaments—from a Hebrew, or Jewish, perspective. Remember, for the first 15 years after Y'shua's resurrection, there were few, if any, Gentile followers of the Jewish Messiah, but there were thousands upon thousands of Jewish disciples, including a great company of Cohanim (priests of Israel) who were obedient to the faith. The Great Commission was to the Jew first, and the Jewish disciples gave their lives to spread the good news of the Messiah to the Gentile world. We are going to let the Jews interpret the Scriptures that the Jews have written ... and on the bottom corner margin of the final page in this book, I have reserved ample room for the Gentiles to interpret all of the Scriptures that the Gentiles have written!

CHAPTER THREE

Patronizing Pagan Parties

In the New Testament, Shimon Kefa [known as Simon Peter in the West] said that haul's [the apostle Paul's] writings are very difficult to understand, and those who are ignorant of the Torah twist his words and end up destroying themselves and the people who listen to their twisted sermons. Shaul constantly quoted the five books of Moses—the same Scriptures that the Bereans searched to prove his teachings.

Despite his repeated warnings, the modern Christian Church has turned a deaf ear to GOD's instructions and has adopted the forms, philosophies, traditions, and rituals of Babylonian sun god worship ... and they call it "Christianity." But just as Jeremiah prophesied, in the last days, the Gentiles will cry out in repentance, "Truly, we have inherited nothing but **lies** from our fathers. We have inherited the worship of **pagan gods**." This day, may this Scripture be fulfilled in our ears ...

In Your Mind's Eye

Words communicate ideas primarily through pictures formed the mind. When I say the word, "Mother," you get a specific picture in your mind. It is not the same picture that I see, but there are similarities. Words also communicate emotion. "Mom" has a different quality and stirs a remembrance that is distinct from "Ma!" or "Mommy!" Once a picture and the associated emotions are fully developed in one's mind, no matter how inaccurate they may be, it is extremely difficult for one to see another viewpoint. The *truth* isn't even relevant because the subconscious mind has already pre-judged the issue.

It is not comfortable to consider that the pictures held in one's mind and upon which one bases concepts of truth or reality, might be in error. Let me give you an example.

The Elah Valley, where David slew Goliath.

A Myth About David

David is usually pictured as a little boy with a crotch-stick slingshot going up against the giant Goliath. But David was *not* a little boy at the time. How do we know this?

David took provisions to his brothers who were encamped in battle against the Philistine army. A giant named Goliath, a champion in battle, stood on the other side of the valley and blasphemed the name of the Almighty, challenging any warrior of Israel to a death-match to decide the outcome of the war.

David was infuriated with Goliath's blasphemy, and said that he would accept the giant's challenge. David earned his audience with King Saul because he was proclaiming his resume throughout the camp of Israel and causing quite a stir among the soldiers (1 Samuel 17:1-40). David boasted that the Almighty would deliver Goliath into his hands, because He had delivered David from the other "Goliaths" in his life. He related two incidents that took place when he was a shepherd. A bear came out of the woods and attacked a lamb. David wrestled the bear to the ground, delivered the lamb from its jaws, and beat the bear to death with a club. On yet another occasion, David said he assaulted a lion, grabbed him by the beard, and killed him with his bare hands ... not exactly the description of the physical prowess of a 10-year-old child.

David was not only strong, but also tall. How do we know this? We read that King Saul was "head and shoulders above every man in the kingdom" when he was crowned. He was a big man to whom everyone looked up. Now, several years later, when David wanted to take out this giant

Philistine, Goliath, King Saul compelled David to wear his own royal armor to fight him. David put on the king's full set of armament and cinched Saul's sword around his waist. But before the battle, David requested to be allowed to fight without the armor—not because it didn't fit him, but because he hadn't proved Saul's armor in battle; however, David did know what he could do with a military sling and stone. King Saul's armor had to fit David in order for him to put it on ... or for King Saul to even suggest it!

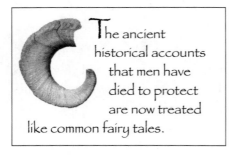

The ancient historical accounts that men have died to protect are now treated like common fairy tales.

David, too, was a big man! David used Goliath's 45-pound iron sword to lop off the giant's head after he broke his skull with a rock. Later, David used the same sword as a personal combat arm. David was a young man of towering stature and powerful physique, and yet he is commonly thought to have been a child at the time he killed Goliath.

Tradition has consistently portrayed the men and women in the Scriptures as one-dimensional cartoon characters. The ancient historical accounts that men have died to protect are now treated like common fairy tales. Numbered sound bytes, called verses, have been wrested completely out of context and interpreted in ways that must make Shaul and Moses roll over in their graves.

We Have Inherited Lies, Vain Worship, and Pagan Gods

Jeremiah said that in the last days, Israel would return to their own land and the Gentiles would come unto the sons of Israel and cry out in repentance, "Surely our fathers have inherited nothing but lies, vain worship, and passed down to us pagan gods ..." Why would they say this? The Almighty said that one day we would ask why so much evil has come upon us, and the answer would be, "It is because your fathers have followed after the ways that the heathen worshipped their gods and they said they were doing it for me. Your fathers forsook my Torah, my instructions, and developed their own religion by following their own imaginations" (Jeremiah 16: 9-21). If our fathers inherited lies, the only things that they can pass onto us are lies. Whether they intended to or not is irrelevant.

In Shaul's letter to the believers in Colossi, he instructs those who have accepted the Messiah, Y'shua, to be very diligent in their endeavor to follow Him. It is stated very poetically in the King James Version of Colossians 2:6:

> As ye have therefore received Christ Jesus the LORD, so walk ye in him ...

The Name of Jesus Christ

It is amusing to hear some people refer to Jesus as though He was the son of Joseph and Mary Christ. *Christ* is a Greek title, not His last name. I prefer to use the Hebrew title, *Mashiach* or "Messiah," in place of the Greek term *Christos* or "Christ," because the Greeks called all their gods, from Adonis to Zeus, *Christos*. It means merely, "anointed." When

I use the term "Messiah," however, I am referring to **THE ONE** of whom Moses spoke when he said, "You **must** listen to **that** prophet."

Being that I am a Jewish follower of the Jewish Messiah, I hope you will bear with me in this matter: I prefer to use the Lord's Hebrew name, Y'shua, rather than His Gentile nickname, Jesus.

I love the name Yahshua. I also use Yeshua, which is the same as saying, "Savior." I commonly use the contracted written English form, Y'shua, for the comfort of those who prefer a different syllabic pronunciation. Yahshua is also

ROOD-imentary Explanation

Y'shua: a common, compound name in Hebrew
(in English, "Joshua")

Where does it come from and what does it mean?

Yah: the short form of the name Yahweh

Yeshua is Hebrew for "salvation"

Yahweh – Yeshua: commonly contracted, Yah-shua:
"Yahweh is our Salvation"

The angel Gavriel instructed Miriam to name her son
Yahshua, for He (Yahweh) will save (Yeshua) His peole
from their sins (Matthew 1:21).

the name of the leader of Israel who brought us into the Promised Land; his name is commonly pronounced as "Joshua." But there is no J sound in the Hebrew or Greek

I love the name Yahshua. I also use Yeshua, which is the same as saying, "Savior."

languages. In fact, there was no J in the English language until 20 years after the King James Version of the Scriptures was first published. The original 1611 version of the King James was written with the letter "Y" accurately supplied for all of the names that began with the Hebrew letter "yod." Throughout the continent of Europe, the letter J is still pronounced as the letter Y. If you pronounce each J in the English versions of the Bible as a Y, then you will be very close to the correct pronunciation of each word.

Our Israel-based television crew was infinitely amused as we filmed a "man on the street" interview for our series. We set up our cameras on the Ben Yehudah pedestrian mall in downtown Jerusalem.

First we found English speakers who were also fluent in Hebrew. We started our "on-camera" interview with the question: "Do you speak Hebrew?"—to which the respondent usually answered in the affirmative in the Hebrew language, "Ken, ani medaber Ivrit."

The next question: "I understand that all Hebrew names have a meaning?"—to which the respondent invariably answered in the affirmative, "Ken (yes)."

The next question: "Since all Hebrew names have a meaning, what is the meaning of the name, *Jesus*?" The responses were priceless. First, the startled look on their faces as they perceived that they were being put on the spot regarding a religious issue. Many of those that we interviewed were orthodox Jews. Then the verbal stumbles that exhibited their desire to give an accurate answer to a very difficult, if not impossible, question.

Finally the truth came out as they struggled for the right words to express ... "Nothing! The name *Jesus* doesn't mean anything in the Hebrew language—Jesus is not a Hebrew name." One young man suggested that Jesus must have been a Mexican because there are hundreds of thousands of Mexicans who are named *Jesus*, but not a single Jew in the history of the world has ever been named, *Jesus*!" Out of the mouth of babes ...

Y'shua, the Messiah

While we are correcting terminology, let me say that I consider myself to be a believer in, and a follower of Y'shua, whom I believe with all my heart, soul, mind, and strength to be the Messiah of the GOD of Avraham, Yitzchak, and Ya'akov. Some think it unusual for a Jew to believe in Jesus, but I think it is amazing that so many Gentiles have become followers of the Jewish Messiah.

Christians often forget that during the first 15 years of what many call the "Christian Church," there were few, if any, Gentiles in the body of believers; not until the mention of Cornelius, a righteous Roman centurion, do we hear of any by name. These Jewish believers were the ones who gave their lives to get the good news of the Messiah out to the Gentile world.

Gentiles in Antioch first referred to other Gentile followers of the Messiah as "Christians." That is **not** what the believers were called back in Jerusalem. And with the morbid history that followed many of those who called themselves "Christians," it is understandable that Jewish believers often distance themselves from such negatively charged labeling. Let me be known simply as a "follower of the Messiah," Y'shua the Nazarene, the only begotten Son of the Living God.

Shaul's Warning to Gentile Believers

Shaul's words are written to all followers of the Messiah, but his warning is specifically to Gentiles raised in the midst of the pagan sun god worshipping culture of Colossi.

> *Beware lest any man **spoil** you through **philosophy** and vain deceit, by following after the tradition of men, and following after the rudiments of the world, and not following after Messiah ... (Colossians 2:8).*

Shaul said very clearly, "**You** who have accepted the Messiah are responsible to **follow** him. You are to be wary—watch your back, lest any man spoil you ..." The word, "spoil," is a military term. When an army conquers a city, all of the possessions that the inhabitants have acquired through a lifetime of toil immediately become "spoil" for the conquerors. The "any man," to whom Shaul refers, is the collective "men" of the pagan culture of Colossi. These

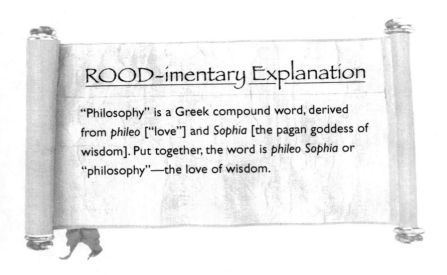

ROOD-imentary Explanation

"Philosophy" is a Greek compound word, derived from *phileo* ["love"] and *Sophia* [the pagan goddess of wisdom]. Put together, the word is *phileo Sophia* or "philosophy"—the love of wisdom.

were Gentiles who were separated from the covenants of Israel, and had no hope in the true GOD. These are the men who would conquer and "spoil" the believers by two means: philosophy and vain deceit.

Now, there is nothing wrong with wisdom. In fact, Solomon asked for wisdom from the Almighty and was rewarded with righteous wisdom, as well as vast wealth. In direct contrast, however, the Greek concept of wisdom has its roots in the worship of fallen angels. The essence of Greek philosophy is the expression of one's "worldview" ... whatever that happens to be.

Do You Have Any Idea Why We're Here?

After the basics of food, shelter, and clothing are satisfied, the primary need of man is to understand why he is here. "What is this conscious physical experience we call *life?*"

As intelligent beings, we need a reason to *be* and a mechanism for our existence. Animals have no such intellectual drive. A cow is content merely to be milked. And if man can be misled into constantly chasing better food, better shelter, and better clothing, his comfort becomes the main purpose of life. He eventually develops the philosophy, "He, who dies with the most toys, wins." He will degrade into a simple, tax-paying consumer who will get "milked" all the way to the grave, never understanding the purpose of our existence. When the whir of constant entertainment subsides, those who have not settled the question of life cry out in the darkness of personal desperation: "Who am I, and why am I here?"

When one admits that he does not know the meaning of life, and he does not know whether or not there is a Creator with a plan for the universe, he refers to himself as "agnostic." This is the haunting admission that he simply does not know. Truly, he does not "know" the Creator of life.

"Atheists" have a more refined philosophy or worldview. They envision a cosmos in which there is no GOD. They are no longer haunted by the questions that torment agnostics as they continue to search for meaning. Atheists have a religion that comforts them: It is called, "Evolution." Evolution answers the question of how we got here without there being a Creator to whom we are responsible. But, evolution is a religion that lacks any shred of evidence in the scientific world, and in fact, breaks several of the proven Laws of Science (including the second law of thermodynamics). But faith doesn't require facts in the religion of Evolution. It is based in the worldview that there is no Creator, and no amount of evidence will shake those who find solace in ignorance and comfort in denial. Their greatest hope is that

ROOD-imentary Explanation

AGNOSTIC
In Greek – *a*, meaning "without" and *gnostic*,
meaning "knowledge"
Agnostic – "without knowledge"
This is a haunting admission that he simply does
not know the purpose of life or the reason for his
existence. Truly he does "not know" the Creator
of Life.

ATHEIST
In Greek – *a*, meaning "without" and *theos*,
meaning "god"
Atheist – "without GOD"

there is no enduring consciousness or soul. When they die, they hope that they are truly dead for all eternity!

For an atheist, there is no commandment or responsibility to **not** murder, steal, rape, or fornicate with animals. **Do what thou wilt** is the only commandment of the religion taught in the public schools of America today. American Christians did not heed the words of Shaul. They were **not** wary of the philosophies of the heathen, and they were eventually conquered and spoiled by their worldview and by the rampant lawlessness that comes from their twisted, atheistic concept of reality.

The Believer's Rights, Responsibilities, and Rewards

I, too, have a philosophy—a worldview. It is succinctly expressed in Shaul's letter to the Messianic Hebrews, chapter 11, verse 6:

> GOD *is, and He is a rewarder of them that diligently seek Him (Hebrews 11:6).*

America was founded upon the principle that all men are created by GOD with "absolute rights" that no politician, priest, or king has the authority to strip from the individual. We published that "Unanimous Declaration" to the entire world on July 4, 1776. At the time of the founding of this unique republic, Americans unanimously agreed that among these GOD-given rights, was the right to pursue happiness. The founding fathers suggested that pursuing **GOD's will** for our individual lives is the essence of the happiness that we have the right to **diligently seek.** Just as our "Unanimous Declaration" of July 4, 1776 proclaims, **true Americans** believe in the Creator and in Creator-given rights. In fact, the founding fathers taught that men must govern themselves as individuals according to GOD's Ten Commandments. With GOD-given rights come GOD-given responsibilities ... not "**do what thou wilt,**" the philosophy of the atheist. And, by the way, "**do what thou wilt**" is the first and only commandment inscribed in the satanic bible.

Let's Continue With Shaul's Warning

> *Beware lest any man spoil you through philosophy and **vain deceit**, by following after the tradition of men, and following after the rudiments of the*

*world, and not **following after Messiah** ...*

The word "**vain**" in the King James Version of the Bible can most effectively be translated into the vernacular as "**prosperity.**" It is the pursuit of **things** that so easily **deceive** us.

We read in the Gospel of Matthew that Satan tempted the Messiah with all the power, wealth, and glory of the world. Satan offered to give it to Him if He would simply worship at his feet (Matthew 4:8-10). This is the same carrot that Satan and his emissaries continue to hang before the noses of the believers: promises of wealth and power that can, of course, be used for the glory of GOD, but the pursuit of which keeps us chasing the dream and from truly **following after Messiah.**

Beware lest any man spoil you through philosophy and vain deceit, by following **after** the tradition of men, and following **after** the rudiments of the world, and not following **after** Messiah ...

The word "**after**" can be used as a position in time, such as, "**After** I make my fortune, I will search for the meaning of life." Or "after" can be used as a position in place or rank, such as, "following **after** the Messiah." In this context, we see that "after" is used as "position in place." Those who had accepted the Messiah were to be very careful to follow **after Him,** and to be wary of the pagans who would conquer them with their twisted worldview and cause them to chase after the riches that the world offers.

How would this deception occur? By innocently *following after* the **traditions** of men. The English word, "**tradition,**" is derived from the Latin *tradiere*, which means, "to lay into the hands of another." Tradition can be good or evil; the recipient must carefully inspect that which is laid into his hands. We are warned that by following after the traditions of these pagans, we set ourselves up to be stripped of the reward for which we have worked an entire lifetime.

Welcome to the Pagan Party!

Let's look at **one** of these pagan traditions that have destroyed the lives of innumerable Christians who thought that they were following the Messiah.

We read in the scroll of Ruth that Elimelech and his family left Bethlehem during a drought and sojourned east of Israel in the land of Moab. The Moabites were worshippers of Chemosh, the pagan god of prosperity. It was the same cast-iron, pot-bellied god that their kindred, the Ammonites, worshipped by the name of Molech. Both gods wore the Phrygian cap—the official headwear of both Tammuz in Babylon, and later, Mithra in Rome.

At the time of the Winter Solstice, December 25th on the ancient calendar, they had a public child mass [*mass* meaning "sacrifice"]. The priests stoked the iron image of the enthroned Chemosh with wood and burning pitch, turning their pot-bellied god into a cherry red furnace. The people made long lists of their desires, and recited them to the god of prosperity just before they put their infant children into the red-hot lap of their god with his Phrygian cap. As the babies were incinerated in the December 25th child mass, the people were assured that their sacrifices would be rewarded in the coming year.

> As the babies were incinerated in the December 25th child mass, the people were assured that their sacrifices would be rewarded in the coming year.

On the same day, south of Israel, the Egyptians worshipped their sun god, Ra. An Egyptian hieroglyph depicts Ra castrating himself—the same act that Greek mythology attributes to Attis. Worshippers of Ra would hang gold and silver balls on an upright palm tree, as the prophet Jeremiah reports, and place their decorated gifts to the sun god under the tree adorned with the gold and silver testicles of Ra (Jeremiah 10:1-5). This vain custom was performed on Ra's birthday—December 25th. When Israel adopted this custom, they used the evergreen tree, which they cut out of the forest with an axe and erected in their homes with the help of a hammer and nails so that it would not topple over. Finally, they decked it with gold and silver balls. The Almighty calls this festival "an abomination." In the 1600s it was illegal to have a Christmas tree, or even a Christmas service, in America. The pilgrims knew that it was pure pagan sun god worship. So, don't be offended that I am telling you these things; be offended that these abominations have gone unchallenged by modern, paganized Christianity!

These occult practices have changed very little since being brought into America. A month before the birthday of Tammuz, we have our children make endless lists to the cherry-red, pot-bellied god of prosperity, and then we place our terrified children in the lap of this god who wears his Phrygian cap and sits on his throne in the shopping mall. On Christmas Eve, he will come down the fireplace chimney and deliver gifts under the evergreen tree decorated with gold and silver balls. Our children will kneel before the evergreen phallic symbol as they receive the blessings from their god.

Parents charge their credit cards to the limit to make certain that their children are not disappointed when their god makes good on his promise of prosperity. Months before the event, the world shifts into high gear to promise the most fulfilling experience of life, when our children open boxes filled with their greatest hopes and dreams ... **more stuff.**

The reality is never as great as the carrot dangled before our noses. Our children are disappointed before the last package is opened, and we are in debt for the next eight months as we try to pay for this sinking feeling of despair. That morning's events set up a chain reaction resulting in the highest incidence of suicide during the entire year. But, instead of literally putting our children into the fiery red hands of Chemosh on Childmass day, we abort millions of babies during the rest of the year, and then celebrate our affluence by lavishing gifts upon business colleagues we don't even like, just to show that the god of prosperity is still smiling on us approvingly. It is the same god that is served; the names of the god just change from culture to culture.

Now you can begin to see why Shaul was so intent on warning us to not *follow after* the **traditions** of the heathen. We start by accepting one seemingly harmless tradition, a tradition which, like yeast, grows until it contaminates our entire world. Now, Christmas day is the biggest movie day in America—we can't wait to escape from the disappointing reality that we have created.

Continuing With Shaul's Warning

> *Beware lest any man spoil you through philosophy and vain deceit, by following after the tradition of men, and following after the **rudiments of the world**, and not following after Messiah ... (Colossians 2: 8).*

"**Rudiments**" are best described as the individual elements that make up the whole, like the bricks in the wall that make up a building. Shaul implies that we can be deceived—one brick at a time—until one day we wake up in a prison we have built for ourselves. We will have followed after the things of this world without even realizing that we have been led away from following the Messiah. We will have been tricked out of our eternal reward. Remember, salvation is by grace—rewards must be earned through obedience and service.

Shaul Warns Repeatedly

Because of our ignorance of the Torah, the first five books of the Bible, we do not realize that Shaul is continually quoting the message of the Torah throughout his writings. In Deuteronomy 12:30, we read the basis of his warning to the Gentile believers:

> Take heed to thyself [or, **You** beware] that thou be not snared [spoiled] by following them [whom? the pagan sun god worshippers]. Thou shalt not inquire how these nations served their gods, and do the same unto YHWH, thy Elohim! Everything they do is an abomination. YHWH hates that they have burned their sons and their daughters as a sacrifice to their gods.

In Exodus 23:13 we read the same warning:

> You be circumspect ... [**You** are responsible to watch all around you; be wary ...] and make no mention of the name of other gods ...

That is how careful we are commanded to be. Not only are we not to follow after the ways in which the heathen worship their gods; we are not even to mention their names. The admonition continues in verse 14:

> ... Three times **thou shalt** keep a feast unto me in the year.

When the Almighty created Adam, He knew that He was creating a *party animal*. But, we have clear instructions regarding how He wants His people to *party*: Three times a year **you shall** have a festival—a feast to Me—in the way *I* prescribe." We are not to learn the ways that the heathen serves his false gods and then adapt them to worship the Holy One. We are not to be contaminated by the stench of their child sacrifice offerings or their pagan prosperity gospel.

What is the "Therefore" There For?

In Colossians 2:12-15, we are told that when we accept the Messiah, our old sinful ways are to die and we are to become new creations. When we are obedient in baptism, our old man and the sins of our flesh are buried with Him. Colossians 2:16 continues:

> *"Therefore, let no **man** judge you..."*

The word "**therefore**" is a conjunction that references the entire preceding context of Shaul's message to the Colossians and identifies the "**man**" we are **not** to allow to judge us. This "**no man**" belongs to the same group of heathen sun god worshippers who would attempt to capture us with their traditions and steal our rewards: the ones who would snare us with their worldview and systematic deception.

In **what** are we to allow "**no man**" to judge us? Colossians 23:16-17 goes on to state:

> *"... in meat, or in drink, or in respect of an holyday, or of the new moon, or of the Sabbaths—**which are a shadow of things to come** ..."*

Those pagans want to put us under their rules, regulations, and rituals. They want us to follow the way they serve their gods, and get us to follow their traditions so that they can steal our reward from following the Messiah. I will not subject myself to their perverted, disgusting forms of satanic worship. They will not judge me. I have died to their world, and I will not return to the vomit of Tammuz worship. I prefer to celebrate the Feasts of the LORD, just as we were commanded. The Feasts of the LORD are prophetic shadow pictures of good things to come. But if **they** cannot judge me in what I can or cannot eat, or in how I respect the biblical holy days (which are all reckoned by the appearance of the new moon) or in celebrating GOD's Sabbaths, then **who** is to judge?

"...The body of Messiah."

In Colossians 2:17, the King James Version answers the question of **who** is to be allowed to judge us in the festivals in which the believers may participate:

*"... **but** the body **is** of Christ."*

First, the word *"is"* is italicized in the King James Version because the verb *"is"* does not appear in the original text. The translators used italics to tell us when they were adding words to the Holy Writ that were not originally there. In fact, adding the word *"is"* turns the statement into a different issue that confuses the entire topic that Shaul is belaboring. It should read:

*"...**but** the body of Messiah."*

The word **"but"** is a contrasting conjunction. Because of the lengthy list of biblical holidays, which are finally summed up with the overview "which are a shadow of things to come (literally: Divine prophetic shadow pictures)," the English reader often loses track of the subject at hand, which in a broad overview would read something like this:

> *Therefore, let no heathen sun god worshipper judge you in the foods that you do or do not eat, or the festivals that you keep (such as the biblically mandated Feasts that are all prophetic shadow pictures of good things to come in the future).* ***"But,"*** *(if these pagans have no authority to judge how we celebrate these feasts now that the Temple in Jerusalem is destroyed and the Messiah has already fulfilled the Spring Feasts of the LORD, who does have the proper understanding of the Feasts and the authority to decide in such matters? ... The Body of Messiah."*

Spirit-Filled Followers Know the Torah

Yes, the spirit-filled followers of the Messiah, like the Bereans, are not ignorant of the Torah. They alone are qualified to judge how we now celebrate the Feasts of the LORD—the shadow pictures of good things to come. The Temple in Jerusalem is in ruins. The Levitical priesthood is in disarray. But does that mean that I cannot celebrate the Feasts of the LORD, which are the intricate shadow pictures of what the Messiah must fulfill? GOD forbid! Celebrating the Feasts is the most pure, honest, wholesome worship experience afforded the follower of the Messiah. The feasts of the sun god worshippers, on the other hand, are dark shadows of child sacrifice and Babylonian fertility rites.

Shaul closes his exhortation with:

> *"**Therefore**, let no man beguile you [or trick you to spoil you] of your reward ... If your old way of life was buried with the Messiah and you died from following after the rudiments of the world, why are you subjecting yourself to their rules and regulations by **following after the commandments and doctrines of men?**"*

"Get a grip on it!" Shaul says. You are no longer a part of the sick, twisted world of pagan sun god worship, so step into the beauty of the shadow pictures of good things to come, the Feasts of the LORD. It is blasphemous how some Christian teachers categorize the celebration of the Feasts of the LORD as "following after the commandments and doctrines of men" while they are personally celebrating every pagan holiday that came out of Babylon. As the Scriptures record:

> *"... those who are unlearned and ignorant (of the Torah, the basic instructions from the Creator) wrestle Shaul's words to their own destruction. (II Peter 3:15-16) MIV**

GOD declared the end from the beginning through the shadow pictures embedded in the Feasts of the LORD. The Feasts of the LORD are the foundation of all Bible prophecy, and without knowledge of the Feasts, the Gentiles will never be able to decipher the book of Revelation. The Gospels show how the Messiah fulfilled the Spring Feasts. The book of Revelation shows how the Messiah **will** fulfill the Fall Feasts.

---

* Marine Infantry Version

CHAPTER FOUR

Synchronize Your Babylonian Timepieces

In Shaul's [the Apostle Paul's] first letter to the believers in the city of Thessalonica, chapter 5, verse 1, he wrote,

> *Concerning the **times** and **seasons**, brethren, you have no need that I write to you.*

The Creator's **times** and **seasons** are two distinct concerns. Throughout the Scriptures, the word, "**seasons**," is from the Hebrew word, *moedim*, meaning literally "**appointed times**," which are defined in the 23rd chapter of Leviticus as the Feasts of the LORD. In the Brit Hadesha, or New Testament, they are referred to as "**shadow pictures of good things to come**" (Colossians 2:16-17, Hebrews 10:1). They are sometimes mistakenly called the *Jewish Feasts*.

The Feasts of the LORD are referred to in Leviticus 23 as "Kadosh Mikra" or "Holy Rehearsals" that the Israelites were to keep forever. The Almighty did not just forbid the inculcation of pagan festivals into the lifestyle of His people;

He commanded the observance of *His* Feasts as a *rehearsal* of good things to come.

These Feasts belong to the Creator; Israel was simply commanded to observe them. The Feasts did not magically become "Jewish" just because the Jews have been relatively faithful in observing them. The Feasts of the LORD are literally the Creator's method of "telling the end from the very beginning" (Isaiah 46:10). The Feasts are the prophetic shadow pictures of what the Messiah MUST fulfill in order to legally redeem Israel.

The first four Gospels—Matthew, Mark, Luke, and John—depict how Y'shua the Messiah fulfilled the Spring Feasts of the LORD in every detail in which the Nation of Israel rehearsed these Feasts for over a thousand years. Y'shua fulfilled these shadow pictures with absolute accuracy—to the very day, hour, and moment of their rehearsed times. The fifth Gospel, the book of Revelation, details how the Messiah **WILL** fulfill the Fall Feasts of the LORD with the same exactness and precision in which He fulfilled the Spring Feasts.

Without an understanding of the Spring Feasts of the LORD, the Gospels will remain shallow and confusing to the Western Gentile reader. Without an understanding of the Fall Feasts of the LORD, the book of Revelation will remain an indecipherable time warp continuum to the Western dispensational prophecy gurus who continually paint the end times canvas vacated of pew warming Christians who have no desire to participate in the most exciting time in the history of the human race: the latter rain outpouring of the Holy Spirit and the end time harvest.

*Concerning the **times** and **seasons**, brethren, you have **no need that I write to you**.*

The "**times**" of which Shaul speaks refer to the Creator's reckoning of time, which is clearly detailed in the Hebrew Scriptures. Why did Shaul indicate there was no need for instruction on these things? These first century Jewish followers of the Messiah conducted their lives by the Creator's reckoning of time, and were instructed in the Feasts of the LORD from their youth. At the time that Shaul's letter was written, no one could comprehend that in the future, the entire world of commerce would be run on a pagan calendar. But 2,000 years ago, Rome ruled the world, and the Empire began to force its calendar and its gods upon the people whom they conquered.

Less than thirty years after Shaul penned these words, the Roman General Titus destroyed the Temple and the city of Jerusalem—which was later renamed, "Aeolia Capitolina." Everything Jewish was annihilated, and Rome built temples to their gods on the ruins. But, the Romans were unable to destroy the faith that the dispersed remnant maintained in the GOD of Avraham, Yitzak, and Ya'akov, and in the Messiah. All Jews believed that the Messiah **would** come, and tens of thousands of Jews, including a multitude of Priests, believed that He had **already** come and foretold these very events—the destruction of the Temple and the pillaging of Jerusalem.

Three hundred years after Shaul penned these words, the Emperor Constantine instituted a plan to absorb the followers of the Jewish Messiah into the mainstream of Roman society.

He developed a new religious system that even the most committed sun god worshipers would welcome.

First, Constantine forbade anything "Jewish" in his new religion. He fabricated "another Jesus," a paganized messiah who would be completely acceptable to the heathen. The Messiah's real Hebrew name and Jewish character were almost expunged from the collective memory of mankind for the next 1,600 years. The name above all names was almost erased from the earth by Constantine's initiative to remove everything Jewish from his *new* world religion. He incorporated all of the accoutrements of pagan sun god worship into this new religion, and named himself "Pontifex Maximus," the title of the high priest of paganism.

Constantine sent his mother, Helena, to Jerusalem to select holy sites that could be venerated and staffed by a new clergy class ordained by the Roman government.

Easter Festivities in Jerusalem

The streets of Jerusalem, known as the Via Dolorosa or the "Way of Suffering," lead into an open courtyard where you must carefully walk around the broken remains of pillars that once adorned the entrance to the temple of Aphrodite. Aphrodite is the Roman version of Easter, the Babylonian goddess of fertility. Easter and Aphrodite were worshipped on the first Sun-day after the Vernal Equinox, the day in spring on which there are equal proportions of daylight and darkness.

On Aphrodite (or Easter) Sunday, the worshippers of the Roman sex goddess would make a pilgrimage through the streets of Aeolia Capitolina and crowd their way into

The Rest of Constantine's Story

In the year 326 of the Common Era, after Constantine's so-called "conversion" at Milvian Bridge, he had a coin minted that tells the rest of the story. On the obverse side is Constantine's image. On the reverse side, we see the image of a man who has the whole world in his hands and a halo of the rays of the sun beaming from his face. Many will recognize Constantine's hero by his birth date, as it is recorded in the Encyclopedia Britannica—December 25th—the day of the Winter Solstice on the ancient Roman calendar. Still a mystery? You will surely identify this deity by the inscription encircling the image: *Sol Invict to Commite* ["Committed to the Invincible Sun"] *Sol Invictus Mithra*. Constantine was a worshipper of the Roman sun god, Sol Invictus Mithra, until the day he died. He had his wife and his oldest son murdered, and later, immortalized himself as the reincarnation of the god Apollo. He placed a statue of himself on a pillar high above all of the other gods in Constantinople. Lightning struck the image, and the Burnt Column is still standing today ... but without Constantine's charred image.

this pagan temple bedecked with white lilies. Constantine's mother selected this same site as the "official" burial place of Jesus. The temple of Aphrodite, the "Queen of Heaven," was broken down, and Helena built the Church of the Holy Sepulcher on the same foundation stones.

On Easter Sunday, the pilgrimage of sun god worshippers continued to parade through these same streets and to crowd into the same location to worship Constantine's new "Jesus" and his mother Mary, the new "Queen of Heaven" (instead of Mithra and Aphrodite). The streets that the worshippers of Aphrodite trod are now adorned with the fictitious "stations of the cross" while the streets that Y'shua walked—no thanks to Rome—are buried under forty feet of rubble and 2,000 years of pagan traditions.

Over the next sixteen centuries, most of the Messianic Jews and their Gentile converts were absorbed into the Constantinian Roman culture, or were, like the rabbinic Jews, hunted down, tortured, and killed.

About three city blocks and 1,600 years removed from the temple of Aphrodite, you can now walk into one of many antiquities shops in the old city of Jerusalem and inspect 1800 BC images of Easter, the Canaanite goddess of fertility. The prophets of Israel cried out against these ancient, pornographic depictions of the "Queen of Heaven," and demanded, in accordance with the Torah, that every one of these images be destroyed. Israel's disobedience is evidenced by the fact that these ancient centerfold models can still be purchased in the city streets of Jerusalem.

Gentile Calendar is Based on Pagan Time

The current world system uses a calendar that was originally developed in Nimrod's Babylon and was later adopted by Rome. It designates the Winter Solstice as the birth date of Tammuz, the reincarnation of Nimrod. It celebrates the Vernal Equinox as the time that Nimrod's wife was reincarnated as Easter, the goddess of fertility. The sun calendar was adopted by Julius Caesar, and updated by Pope Gregory fewer than 500 years ago. The Gregorian calendar begins each day, week, month, and year at a completely fictitious point in time.

The year begins with the first day of January, named after Janus, the two-headed god, and continues the exultation of pagan deities with Februa—the god of purification, Mars—the god of war, Aprilis—a fertility goddess, Maia—the goddess of growth, and June—the wife of Jupiter. July and August are named after men who *became* gods—Julius Caesar and Caesar Augustus. However, September hearkens back to the original Hebrew reckoning of the year; the Latin word *septem* means seventh. September is approximately the time of the seventh Hebrew month, now called Tishri [anciently, *Ethanim*]. *Octo* [October] is eighth, *Novem* is ninth, and *Decem* is tenth. Even though December is the twelfth Roman month, "December" means tenth, and falls at the time of the tenth Hebrew month, now called Chislev.

> If we do not understand the Creator's reckoning of time, we can confuse the Hebrew Scriptures for an entire lifetime.

95

Defining "Day"

To understand the Creator's reckoning of time and His Seasons or Festivals, we must first ask the question, "When does the **day** begin?" The Hebrew Scriptures record, and the Jewish people have faithfully observed, that the **day** begins at sunset, not at the man-made hour of twelve o'clock midnight—a moment in time that was calculated as the point at which the Babylonian sun god was directly opposite one's position on the Earth—a point that is discernable only with the help of a modern chronometer.

Defining "Week"

The **week** begins at sunset at the **end** of the seventh day, the end of the **Sabbath**, the only day of the week that is named in the Bible. All other days are numbered. When the sun sets at the end of the Sabbath, it is the first day of the week; and shops around Jerusalem begin to open their doors for business.

In the book of "The Acts of the *Jewish* Apostles," chapter 20, versus 7-12, we read that the disciples got together early "on the first day of the week" to break bread. They did not get up early on Sunday morning for a sunrise pork and pancake breakfast. They did that which we still do in the Land of Israel: As the sun begins to set at the end of the Sabbath, we gather in homes to

They did not get up early on Sunday morning for a sunrise pork and pancake breakfast.

share a meal with others in the community. We call it "the third meal of the Sabbath [or Shabbat]." Everyone comes with something to share: food, a song, a teaching, or a revelation from the Scriptures. When the sun sets, it is "early the first day of the week," and the fellowship often continues into the early hours of the morning.

It was after the third meal of Shabbat that Shaul started teaching. At about midnight, a sleepy young man fell out of a third story window. Now it is commonly taught among Gentiles that Shaul had been teaching for 18 hours, since the 6 a.m. Sunday sunrise service! That is nonsense!!! Let's consider this Scripture in the light of the culture in which it was written.

After the third meal of Shabbat, the boy fell asleep and plummeted to his death. Shaul, being somewhat responsible for killing the lad, prayed for him, and he was raised from the dead. No one could go to sleep then, so they continued until sunrise when they took Shaul to meet his boat. Then everyone went to work as usual on the first day of the workweek, which was known in pagan cultures as the "day of the sun," or Sunday. That morning on the first day of the week (not "Moon-day," the **second** day), Shaul and his company left for their next adventure. This was standard travel practice that allowed as much time as possible to reach one's destination before the next Shabbat.

Defining "Month"

When does the biblical month begin? It begins with the visible sighting of the first sliver of the new moon. Modern day astronomers have appropriated the term, "new moon," and applied it to an astronomical event that can only be determined by mathematics: the moment at which the moon is in conjunction with the Earth. But the biblical and historical definition of "new moon" is determined when the first sliver of the new moon becomes visible just over the horizon after the sun sets. This is the first day of the month—or "moonth."

The moon continues to wax full night after night until mid-month, and then it wanes until there is no visible moon (after about 27 days). The new moon will reappear 29 or 30 days after the previous new moon. Because the lunar cycle is approximately 29.530587 days long, there will not be a month shorter than 29 days or longer than 30 days. If it is too cloudy to see the moon on the 29th day, then sunset at the end of the 30th day is declared to be the beginning of the new month.

The sighting and certifying of the new moon is an event that must take place in the land of Israel within a one-day walk of the city of Jerusalem. Jerusalem is the place from which the yearly and monthly calendar cycles are to be determined by those to whom it was entrusted: the children of Israel.

When the moon disappeared at the end of the month, everyone would watch the western horizon on subsequent nights, just above the setting sun, for the first glimpse of the new moon. When it was sighted, men would rush up to the Temple Mount to certify the sighting. Long distance travel was ordinarily forbidden on the Sabbath, but when the new moon was sighted on the Sabbath, lengthy travel was

The first sliver of the new moon appears in the sky over Jerusalem.

encouraged and rewarded so that we might properly observe the correct days for the Feasts of the LORD.

The first witnesses normally arrived at night, but the gate to the Temple was shut at sundown. They stood at the gate and called out to the Temple guard, "We have sighted the new moon." The Temple guard verified that at least two witnesses were present before he summoned a member of the Sanhedrin, the ruling body of Israel. Nassi, one of the ruling princes, made diligent inquiry of the first two witnesses, and when the sighting was certain, he gathered the elders into the hall of hewn stones adjacent to the Temple, and then alerted the Cohen Gadol (High Priest). The Cohen Gadol stood on the Temple Mount and cried out to the two witnesses below, "Come up hither! Come up here!" The gate swung open, and the two witnesses ascended the Temple Mount and appeared before the High Priest and elders to declare their sighting of the new moon.

When both witnesses gave the confirming evidence, the Cohen Gadol cried out, "Sound the trumpets!" The trumpets blasted from the Temple Mount, and the sentry posted across the Kidron Valley Bridge on the Mount of Olives put his torch to a well-prepared stack of wood. A pillar of fire and a cloud of smoke ascended from the signal fire, and the sentry sounded his shofar to announce the Rosh Chodesh, the New Month. From mountaintop to mountaintop throughout the land of Israel, the sentries saw the distant signal fires and lit their own fires and blew their shofars to announce to the Nation that the new month had begun.

Defining "Year"

When does the year begin on the Creator's calendar? Establishing the beginning of the year requires another two-fold witness. First, the barley must be "aviv." The barley on the Mount of Olives was first planted there over 3,000 years ago by the Priests of Israel, and continues to reseed itself century after century. This is the location that we still check to find the aviv barley each spring. The new moon immediately following the finding of aviv barley will be declared the Rosh Chodesh (Head of the Month) of the aviv. The Month of the Aviv Barley is the biblical Rosh Ha Shana (Head of the Year) and the month in which we are commanded to celebrate Passover. The Pharisees later changed Rosh Ha Shana to the first day of the seventh month so that they might obscure the prophetic shadow pictures embedded in "Yom Teruah" (the Day of Trumpets) that proclaims the role of the true Messiah. Contrary to rabbinic tradition, Israel was commanded to celebrate Yom Teruah on the first day of the seventh month—not Rosh Ha Shana!

The Torah commands us in the 16th chapter of Deuteronomy:

> *Shamor et Chodesh **Ha'Aviv** ve'asita Pesach la YHWH Elohecha ...*
>
> *Keep the Month of **The Aviv** [barley] and perform the Passover sacrifice to YHWH your GOD ...*

Notice that in the Hebrew text, the accurate term is **"Ha'Aviv"** or **"The Aviv."** The definite article **"Ha"** or **"The"** is always present in the Hebrew text because aviv is not the name of the month, but aviv refers to the level of maturity of the barley crop. The remainder of the verse one reads:

> *... for in the month of **The Aviv** [barley] the LORD thy GOD brought thee forth out of Egypt by night (Deuteronomy 16:1b).*

We are also taught in Exodus:

> *... seven days shall you eat unleavened bread, as I have commanded you, at the time of the month of **the Aviv** [barley], because in the month of **the Aviv** did you go out of Egypt (Exodus 34:18).*

The Aviv

We are commanded to keep Hag Ha Matzot, the Feast of Unleavened Bread, in the *Month of the Aviv*. The term, "the aviv," is an ancient Hebrew agricultural term. The ninth chapter of Exodus relates that the barley in Egypt was destroyed by the plague of hail because the barley was "in the ear," according to the King James translators. But in actuality, the Hebrew text literally reads that the barley was destroyed because it was "**aviv**." So the question remains, what is "aviv barley?" The Hebrew Bible gives us three clues as to the meaning of the agricultural term, "aviv."

Clue #1 – Parched With Fire

The first clue is found in Leviticus 2:14, which says, "**aviv parched in fire**" was offered as a Firstfruits offering. To identify the meaning of Aviv, tests were carried out to determine at which stage in the barley's development it could be parched in fire and still produce food. Barley was gathered in different stages of development and parched in fire. "Green ears of corn," as described in the King James Version, were underdeveloped and incinerated in the heat. This could hardly have been the "**aviv parched in fire**" offered in the Temple.

Clue #2 – Ready to Harvest

The second clue is found in Leviticus 23:10 and Deuteronomy 16:9: The wave-sheaf offering brought during the Feast of Unleavened Bread must be brought from the first sheaf of the harvest. In other words, there must be fully harvestable barley in time for the Feast of Unleavened Bread, fifteen days into the month. Therefore, aviv can be identified as the stage in the barley's development that is two weeks away from being harvestable.

Clue #3 – Damaged When Struck With Hail

The third clue is found in Exodus 9:31-32. The barley was destroyed by hail "because it was aviv." The "slap test" was invented to determine the stage at which the barley becomes brittle enough to be damaged when struck with hail.

The evidence of all three biblical clues points to the same stage of maturity: When the barley seeds are firm like soft cheese, they produce edible grain through parching. At the same stage, the stalks are brittle enough to be damaged when struck by hail, and in about two weeks from that point of maturity, the grain will be ready to harvest.

The Hebrew Calendar: GOD's Time

In 1997, I published the first astronomically corrected biblical Hebrew calendar since the destruction of Jerusalem

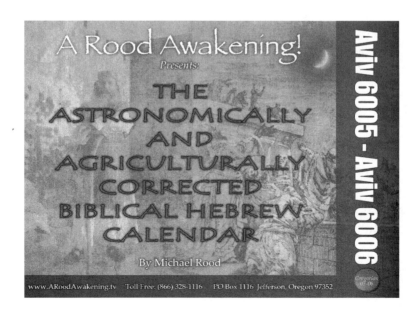

in 70 AD. Nearly two thousand years ago, the remaining tribes of the children of Israel were evicted from the Land. The entire system of sighting and signaling the beginning of the months and years was in disarray. The need for a calculated calendar arose because it had become difficult to inform people scattered over three continents in an accurate and timely manner.

In the year 359 of the Common Era, the Pharisee leader Hillel II invented a pre-calculated calendar to replace the biblical calendar. Using ancient Babylonian mathematical and astronomical charts, he calculated the lunar cycle so that Jews could keep the Feasts on the same day on three continents. Those calculations, while extremely precise, were not accurate enough to keep the projected calendar on track over the long duration in which it has been in use. Now, 1,600 years later, we find ourselves celebrating the Feast Days on the wrong days ... most of the time. Instead of proclaiming the Feasts of the LORD in **their** season, the Pharisees proclaim the Feasts at **their** convenience, according to **their** contrived calendar. But, who cares? We just want to be told what to do by a "self-appointed" religious authority ...

Confirming Time With Barley

Jewish scholars all agree that the original reckoning of time was based on the visible sighting of the new moon and the aviv barley in the land of Israel. Yet there is only one group who has attempted to remain faithful to the ancient practice—the Karaites.

On the other hand, the Rabbinites, who claim to be direct spiritual descendents of the Pharisees, adopted

ROOD-imentary Explanation

"Karaite" comes from the old Hebrew word, *Qara* ["Hebrew Scriptures"]. The term, "Karaite," literally means "Hebrew Scripturalist," and it is applied to those Jews who follow the Hebrew Scriptures without addition or subtraction, as opposed to the Rabbinites who claim authority to add to or subtract from the Scriptures at will.

the innovations of the rabbis laid down in the Talmud (a compendium of Jewish legal discussions, decisions, and commentaries). The Rabbinites adopted the new calculated calendar of Hillel II, while the Karaites remained faithful to the original Hebrew calendar throughout the Middle Ages.

Since the time that we entered the Promised Land with Joshua, we inspected the barley to determine the beginning of the year. The details surrounding the planting and harvesting of the barley for the Firstfruit Offering, were precise and rigorous.

The Book of Psalms mentions the steps leading up to the Holy Temple in the Shir Ha-Ma'alot, the Songs of Steps, sometimes translated as "Songs of Degrees." It was on these very steps that the Aviv Court convened to examine samples of barley and to consider whether the barley had reached the stage of ripening known as "aviv." If the barley was found to be aviv, the next new moon would be declared the month of the Aviv and the "Head of the Year." However, if the barley was **not** yet ripe enough, an announcement would be sent throughout the world that an additional month had been added to allow the barley to ripen. This was the practice at the time of the Second Temple.

One ancient account tells of an actual Aviv announcement issued by the Pharisee leader, Gamliel the First (the same Gamliel mentioned in the 22nd chapter of the Book of Acts as the teacher of Shaul). Gamliel was one of the most prominent Pharisees at the time of the Second Temple. The report reads, "Gamliel was sitting on the steps of the Temple Mount, and [he instructed his scribe, Yochanan] ... Write to our brethren, the Exiles of Babylonia and to those in Media, and to all the other exiled [sons] of Israel, saying: 'May your peace be great forever! We beg to inform that ... **the ripening of the aviv has not yet arrived.** It seems advisable to me and my colleagues to add ... [a month] to this year.'"

No More Need to Calculate?

Throughout the Middle Ages, the Karaites continued to observe the Aviv-New Moon calendar. Karaites in the Middle East sent messengers to the Land of Israel every year to inspect the barley crops. Scattered in exile throughout the distant lands, they used calculations to approximate the time of the aviv, but even then, they did not entirely forsake the true calendar. Whenever travelers arrived in these remote regions with news of the Aviv from the Holy Land, the local Karaites would immediately correct the calendar, even if this meant changing the expected schedule of holy days in the middle of the year!

Even after the destruction of the Temple, all Jews continued to follow the true biblical calendar, using the Aviv and the New Moon to determine GOD's appointed times. But three centuries after their exile, Hillel established a 19-year cycle in which seven years would selectively receive a 13th month. This invented cycle kept Passover at about the right time, but not necessarily in the month of the Aviv. This and other Pharisaic innovations eventually split the Jews into two camps: the Karaites and the Rabbinites.

Even though some would argue that this calculated calendar may have been necessary during our exile, now that we are back in the land, I maintain that there is no reason that we cannot return to GOD's original  reckoning of time, and celebrate the Feasts of the LORD in **their** appointed time. I believe that the Almighty rules the universe according to His reckoning of time—not ours!

Aviv Calendar and Marriage Vows

The Karaites have even incorporated the observance of the Aviv Calendar into the marriage ceremony. To this very day, every marrying couple takes a solemn oath to observe the true biblical calendar. The oath is inscribed in every Karaite ketubah, or marriage contract. In it, the couple swears, "by the covenant of Mount Sinai ... to observe the holy appointed times of YHWH according to the sighting of the New Moon and the finding of the Aviv in the Holy Land of Israel." This same formula can be found in Karaite ketubot, dating back over 1,000 years. By making this vow, the marrying couple expresses their loyalty to the Torah and enters as full adult members into Karaite society. The marriage ceremony of my wife Judith and me was performed in the ancient portico of Jaffa Gate in the Old City of Jerusalem. At that time, we entered into the traditional Karaite covenant to observe the Feasts of YHWH according to the ancient biblical method of reckoning time. Centuries ago, a form of this same vow was incorporated into the standard Karaite liturgy. Even now, on every High Holiday, the Karaite cantor recites the vow, and the entire congregation responds with a resounding, "Emet!" "Truth!"

An Abomination Celebrated in the Modern Jewish Calendar

Originally the Hebrew months were all numbered. During the Babylonian captivity, names were attached to the months. The first month was named Nisan, which has nothing to do with aviv barley. The fourth month was named Tammuz. Ezekiel said that there were women in the Temple committing an abomination: They were weeping for Tammuz. Who is Tammuz, and why is a month on the modern Jewish calendar named after him?

Quick Review of Tammuz

According to Babylonian tradition, when Nimrod was slain, he ascended into Heaven and became the sun god. Nimrod's widow became pregnant by the "rays of the sun" so the story goes, and she delivered her re-incarnated husband Nimrod on the day of the Winter Solstice on the ancient calendar—

December 25th. She named this re-born sun god Tammuz. But, why were women weeping for Tammuz? Tammuz was gored to death by a wild boar in a hunting accident in the 40th year of his life. Each year thereafter, worshippers of the sun god set aside 40 days, one day for each year of his life, in which they would "mourn for Tammuz" by denying themselves a pleasure in this life for the pleasure of Tammuz in the afterlife.

The entire sun god worship season was finalized after Tammuz's mother, the widow of Nimrod, died and was returned to the Earth in a giant egg, which landed in the Euphrates River and cracked open. Out emerged Nimrod's wife reincarnated as Easter, the bare-breasted goddess of fertility who turned a bird into an egg-laying rabbit to proclaim her divinity. Easter Sunday was named in honor of this event. The forty days of "weeping for Tammuz" concluded by slaughtering a wild boar representing the one that killed Tammuz, and eating *ham* on Easter Sunday.

Relatively few of the pagan practices of the month of Tammuz remain in modern Judaism, but Constantine adapted most of the abominations surrounding the worship of the sun god into what is now modern Christianity. Even the sign of Mithra—the Babylonian Tau [or cross of Tammuz]—decorated the banners of the Roman legions a hundred years before the birth of Y'shua. Jews were crucified by the thousands on the cross of Mithra in the city streets of Jerusalem. They were crucified as sacrificse to the Roman sun god. This is the emblem that Constantine chose to designate his new religion, the same emblem that had decorated Roman battle banners for four centuries of conquests.

The Feasts of the LORD

When we comprehend that we have inherited pagan sun god festivals, we also understand that the Christian world has forsaken the Feasts of the LORD, which the New Testament declares to be "prophetic shadow pictures of good things to come." The Feasts of the LORD are the rehearsals embedded in the Hebrew culture, by which GOD declared the end from the very beginning. Having forsaken these specific, prophetic shadow pictures that the Messiah MUST fulfill, we find that it is as if the hands have been broken from the face of the clock. We are lost in time.

Yochanan [John] was a first century Jewish follower of Y'shua of Nazareth whom he believed to be the Jewish Messiah. It is in his recorded Gospel that we read:

> *I have not written everything that could be written, or should be written. The world wouldn't even be able to contain the scrolls of the things that should be written about Y'shua of Nazareth ... But this I have written, that you might know that Y'shua of Nazareth is the Messiah, the only begotten Son of GOD, and that believing, you might have life through his name (John 20:30-31; 21:25).*

How does a Jewish disciple of the Messiah prove to the Jewish people in his culture that Y'shua is the Messiah? What evidence does he use? Of all the things that he could have written, and if the world were large enough, should be written, what incidents does he select to prove that Y'shua is Messiah?

Replica of the Tabernacle in the wilderness.

John shows how Y'shua of Nazareth fulfilled every nuance of the Spring Feasts of the LORD, just as they had been rehearsed every year, century after century, for more than a thousand years. All males of Israel thirteen years and older were required to go up to Jerusalem three times a year to the Pilgrim Feasts. They were to go up to Mount Moreh-Yah, the mountain where Yahweh, the GOD of Israel, would be their Moreh [teacher]. At Mount Moreh-Yah, they would rehearse the coming of the Messiah. Each one of these Feasts was a prophetic shadow picture. Every year, each one of the Feasts was attended with an expectation that "this could be the feast when the Messiah will be revealed." They would come to Jerusalem early to purify themselves in the waters of the *mikveh* (baptismal pool) before the festivities began—hoping, expecting, and praying that maybe this would be the year.

We see that the Gospel of John details how Y'shua of Nazareth fulfills every detail of the Spring Feasts just as they had been rehearsed for thousands of years. That is the reason that the Gospel of John cannot be fully understood from a Western Gentile perspective—because it is 2,000 years removed and many cultures away from a practical understanding of the Feasts of the LORD. Near the end of his life, John wrote the Book of Revelation, in which he detailed how the Fall Feasts of the LORD will be fulfilled to the very day, the very hour, and the exact moment ... just as they have been rehearsed for thousands of years.

Unless we understand the Feasts, we really can't see the beautiful details in the fulfillment of the shadow pictures in the Gospel of John. As a consequence, the Book of Revelation will remain incomprehensible to the Western Gentile Christian mind. Forty years after Messiah fulfilled the Spring Feasts, the temple was destroyed, the Levites went into exile, and all of the rehearsals on the Temple Mount came to an abrupt halt. From that time to this very day, traditions have replaced the rehearsals that the nation of Israel carefully maintained for thousands of years. But for the Messiah, this was not an unexpected turn of events. Y'shua prophesied of the destruction of the Temple and knew that the rehearsals would soon come to a close. During His earthly ministry, He **fulfilled** the Spring Feasts and also **interpreted** the Fall Feasts in a very clear and precise manner so that we would joyfully anticipate their fulfillment in the last days. In fact, He prophesied of the very day that the "Latter Rain" outpouring of the double portion of the Holy Spirit would occur. But, without an understanding of the Feasts of the LORD, we just read on by—rarely lifting a questioning eyebrow.

When you see the fulfillment of the Feasts of the LORD within the pages of the Gospel records, and view the Hebrew Scriptures from a more original Jewish perspective, there will be an explosion in your mind, and your perception will be changed forever. You will **understand**. In Greek, **"understand"** is *sunesis*, meaning "the point at which two streams come together and form a powerful river" (Luke 2:47). You may have studied the Scriptures for an entire lifetime and still have a million streams of disjointed information coursing through the neuron chains in your brain. Understanding the Feasts of the LORD will connect thousands of those streams into a whole new way of being.

Furthermore, there is nothing that you will be able to do about it. When streams begin to flow into rivers in your mind, you will experience a deep and powerful flow of the Spirit of the Living GOD into the depths of your soul. You will be compelled by your own heart to change the way you live and the way you relate to others. Your friends will most likely despise any change you make, because it implies that there is more to life than what they are experiencing.

But all of your life you have hoped that there was more. You have felt out of place and alone so many times, like a cat in a room full of dogs. You may have sat in the same pew for 40 years, listening to the same rehashed theological drivel for the billionth time and fighting the depressing thought that you are missing the whole point of life. That's over. But be fairly warned; you will only get as much truth as you will obey. At the point that you compromise, you cease from "the narrow path that leads to life," and take a left turn into the path "ever learning, but never coming to a knowledge of the truth."

The truth must be lived, and perhaps now you are beginning to understand just how to do so. Walk with patience and perseverance; we are going to be traveling down this road for the rest of our lives.

Remain faithful to the end, and I will see you when the smoke clears ...

Michael Rood

Also by Michael Rood

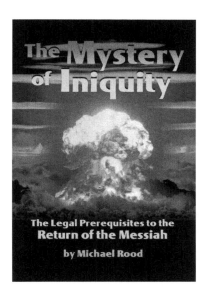

The Mystery of Iniquity

Satan's long war with God will play out in our lifetime. Just as God shook the earth in the days of Noah, He will shake it again. But not just the earth. This time, God will shake the heavens, as well. Impending war. It's coming!

For more information about Michael Rood and the
A Rood Awakening! TV series, go to
www.ARoodAwakening.tv